THE HAPPY LAND

THE HAPPY LAND

by

HOWARD DENTON
and
JIM C. WILSON

THE RAMSAY HEAD PRESS
EDINBURGH

First published in 1991 by
The Ramsay Head Press
15 Gloucester Place
Edinburgh EH3 6EE

ISBN 0 902859 994

The publishers acknowledge
subsidy from The Scottish
Arts Council towards the
publication of this volume.

Printed in Great Britain by
W. M. Bett Ltd, Tillicoultry

Foreword

The title of this book refers as much to a state of mind as to an actual, physical place.

My father came to Scotland in 1900. He had left behind him the very unhappy land of Russian-dominated Poland. In Scotland he was free to work and raise his large family. He was his own boss.

In Edinburgh he lived with many other Jewish immigrants in a maze of tenements between the King's Park and Nicolson Street. That area was known as The Happy Land.

My father would turn his hand to almost anything, just to keep his family fed and clothed. At the age of 12 I was one of his assistants. Since then I have done many jobs, sometimes with hilarious results, in my search to find something which would satisfy me and bring me happiness.

This is the story of a father and a son. Mostly it is a light-hearted tale, but occasionally it is sad. It is also, in part, a story about an old, now mostly demolished, area of Edinburgh, the city which welcomed my father and started each of us on a search for his own version of the happy land.

HOWARD DENTON

Introduction

In 1981 I decided I'd had quite enough of being a Further Education lecturer. So I became a writer.

As the years rolled by, I had a poem published here, a story broadcast there. But something was missing from my life; there was an emptiness. I had no money!

Towards the end of 1985, I spotted a tiny ad in the Personal Column of *The Scotsman*. It said something about a businessman wanting to collaborate with a humorous writer. All very mysterious. I wrote a reply and delivered it to the address, which turned out to be an advertising agency.

Eventually I received a phone call asking me to go to the Country Kitchen restaurant in the West End of Edinburgh. There I met a foreign-looking gent with piercing, hypnotic eyes. He gave me a cup of coffee. He didn't have to buy me one: he owned the restaurant.

As he talked, and I listened, I learned that his interests went far beyond running his business. He seemed to have an almost manic enthusiasm for life. He was in his seventies, but would have passed easily for sixty. He introduced himself to me as Howard Denton, but I learned that he used to be Hyman Zoltie, born into a poor Jewish family in Edinburgh, just before the First World War. Like many immigrants, he had anglicised his name.

He wanted to tell his story, and his father's story. Some of the material was already on paper; some of it was still in his head. I gave him a tape of short stories I'd had broadcast; he gave me some of his hand-written reminiscences to go away and work on. After a couple of weeks we decided to see what we could produce together; some seven months later we had a manuscript entitled *The Happy Land*.

He'd paid me an agreed sum each week, so I had some money, and he had his story. But over the months I'd become more and more engrossed in the life of Howard Denton, and all the many vibrant members of the Zoltie family. I thought the manuscript ought to be published. It was too enjoyable to be left with its pages curling up on some dusty shelf.

So here it is. *The Happy Land*. Read it, and see if you agree with me.

January, 1991   JIM C. WILSON

CHAPTER ONE

Chickens

We were different, and we knew it. We were a Jewish family living in one of Edinburgh's old and smoke-grimed tenement buildings. The name of our narrow, cobbled street was St Leonard's Hill. We were just a few minutes from the Richmond area of the city, where many other Jewish families lived and worshipped. North, South, East and West Richmond Street lay in the shape of a cross and the whole area seemed to me as if it must be one of Auld Reekie's auldest and reekiest parts. With its synagogue and kosher food shops, it was like a little island of foreignness in the centre of Scotland's ancient capital. Many of the Jewish people there were recent arrivals; many spoke very little English. Despite sticking closely together in our over-crowded community, we did not feel threatened by being in a strange place. Edinburgh was notable for the way it readily welcomed and assimilated the Jewish people.

We called the Richmond area The Happy Land; some people have suggested that, strictly speaking, it was only East Richmond Street (now long demolished) that was The Happy Land but I'm sure the term spread to cover the whole Jewish area. I've heard it said that the name was inspired by the fact the Jews were able to live there free from oppression and persecution. I've also heard it claimed that the area was considered a happy one because the Jews and Scots lived peaceably, side by side. Another possible reason is that, because there was such a high concentration of Jews, worship was made easy. To hold a service, there had to be a minyan, ten males over the age of thirteen. Sometimes it was possible to find a quorum within one over-crowded tenement stair. To the many orthodox Jews, that was a welcome state of affairs. But as many of us existed in slum

I

housing and in considerable poverty, I can't help thinking that there was a degree of irony in calling the place The Happy Land.

I said that our family was different. But because of the close proximity of The Happy Land, we didn't feel isolated by our Jewishness. What set our family apart from our neighbours was our noise – and the chickens. My father supplied and cared for his own human brood by travelling the countryside selling anything and everything. I'm sure it was only the weight which stopped him dealing in kitchen sinks. When we were young he went alone and I formed a mental picture of him, a solitary figure silhouetted against the sky as he carried his wares along the roads and lanes from farm to farm, with two large, bulging packs on his back. At first these contained nothing but slippers made by my grandfather, but he eventually increased his stock to include anything people might need. There were pots, pans and pins; he had buttons and elastic and, for the winters, firelighters and hot-water bottles. He even carried the stoppers for kitchen sinks. And when he didn't manage to sell his goods, he simply bartered them for eggs and chickens. And chickens and chickens and chickens.

As our religion demanded that all animals for eating should be ritually slaughtered by the kosher butcher, we were often forced to keep sacks of live chickens at home overnight. The sacks were left in the lobby and, all night long, the squawks and shrieking came through the bedroom door to keep us awake. Unfortunately, the chickens' din also carried out into the communal stairway and into the neighbours' bedrooms. We'd lie awake waiting for the predictable pattern of sounds. First of all, there'd be those of doors opening, one by one, above us and below us. Then, the shuffling of footsteps on the cold, stone stairs, followed by the pounding of a fist on our front door. A click, as Mother opened the latch. Lying there, beneath the cracked and grimy ceiling of the bedroom, I could visualise the gaslit meeting. Mother's warm, round face would be smiling disarmingly at the angry callers but always there would be a noisy torrent of complaints.

2

'What d'ye think is goin' on here? Is it a chicken farm ye've got in there?'

'Chicken farm? Vot do you mean, chicken farm?' came Mother's reply, doubtless followed by a look of wide-eyed innocence. Then the baffled neighbours would retreat along the landing, muttering about noises, chickens and children. Noises, chickens and children; that summed up our family perfectly.

In the morning there might be a new egg at the bottom of the sack. We would grope around in the living frenzy of feathers until we found one. To us it was like a pearl in an oyster; we saw no dry and dusty old sack. My sister Anna particularly liked to hunt among the dark folds, always hoping to discover a brown egg. If she did so, she ran to Mother who would shout, 'Oyee, my Anna,' and place it on the very top of her bowl of eggs. My brothers, Reuben perhaps, and Karl and Motty, would gather round with me, craning to see the prized brown egg. I was Mother's favourite, and knew it. She would push back a strand of her dark hair and smile down at me. Despite having brothers and sisters all around me, Mother, or Kootky as my father liked to call her, was the only person I felt really close to. She was a quiet, wise woman, the centre of my small world. It was as if she sensed I needed just a little bit more care and attention. She made me feel, in the midst of our rough and tumble existence, not unlike the one brown egg among the white.

It was my grisly duty to take the chickens to St Leonard's Street to be slaughtered by the butcher before I went to school in the morning. I had to rush down the steep, winding stairs, with the sack on my back and the demented chickens thrashing and squawking about like a feather mattress gone wild. I scurried out of the dark entry into the grey gloom of early morning. I'd no time to play games with the cracks in the pavement. I wanted to get my onerous chore over and done with, so that I might get myself to school and back to normality. This wasn't because I was a model pupil in love with my lessons but because I just wanted to seem like all the other children. I was already isolated

3

by being the only Jewish boy in my class at St Leonard's Primary School and by having to miss the Christian prayers and hymns which started off every morning. Every day I had to walk in late as the Scottish children stared at me. I felt like a curious exhibit from some strange and distant land.

This isolation made me feel awkward enough but I was also, to my endless embarrassment, the only child there who had to carry sacks of noisy chickens through the streets to be slaughtered. It was a torment to me and I never got used to it.

Now, looking back, it is this image in particular which has remained indelibly with me. I recall the warmth of the feathery bodies pressing through the back of my jacket. And I recall, too, the cold weight of spent carcasses, after the butcher had completed his task.

In later life, I've heard men blame Adolf Hitler for the fact that they smoked or drank. There is one man who, indirectly, is responsible for me having had to carry sacks of chickens through the streets of Edinburgh. That man was the Tsar of Russia.

CHAPTER TWO

Leaving Bialystok

I suppose Tsar Nicholas the Second was a tragic figure, though I find it difficult to sympathise with him. His pitiful assassination put a violent end to his dynasty and allowed the revolutionaries to continue the bloodshed and terror which he and his forebears had inflicted on the Russian people for centuries.

Few felt pity for Nicholas or for Alexandra, the wife who'd been so skilfully and evilly manipulated by Rasputin. Nicholas must have observed the omens: the organised industrial strikes at more and more frequent intervals and the peasants' increasing restlessness after the Acts of Emancipation. The bad harvests, famines and inhuman living and working conditions all contributed to the ferment until there were outbursts of violent rebellion throughout the provinces. The old order was crumbling.

Rumours of this strife and unrest eventually reached a little tobacconists's shop in the old town of Bialystok in Russian-dominated Poland. Travellers arrived from over the border almost daily with their tales of disturbances and open revolt. The owners of the shop quickly realised that troubled times could lie ahead for them.

That shop was run by Maurice Zoltie, my father, along with his two brothers, Karl and Hyman. They made a living out of it but the dark news from over the border gave them second thoughts about the security of their futures in the old town, and in Poland.

Karl was the oldest of the three and an aggressively hard-working businessman. Hyman, the youngest, was more easy-going and tolerant, more a thinker than a man of action. Maurice, my father, seemed to come somewhere 'in between' his brothers in nature as well as age. He was good-natured and

5

likeable although he looked fierce, being six feet two inches in height, with a warlike moustache. He was broad as well as tall, and had strong, dark features. He had grown up on the other side of Asia in Vladivostok on the shore of the icebound Sea of Japan. But the family had travelled the thousands of miles from East to West on the Trans-Siberian railway and the brothers had gone to work in the fields around Bialystok. Hard toil and saving had earned them their tobacconist's shop where they not only sold but made the cigarettes. The leaves came from the Balkan shores far to the south, and the brothers spent many long hours rolling their perfect cigarettes in the back shop. As they worked, they must have discussed the threatening political situation. My father who could at times be a stubborn man, would have preferred to ignore the rumours which were filtering through and just get on with business. My uncles, however, realised that the talk wasn't empty gossip. And if Russians were going to suffer you could be sure that the Jews would have it even worse. History had proved that inevitable.

Bialystok was a reasonably tolerant community. The Christians there had learned to live alongside their Jewish neighbours with their very different customs and rituals. But it wasn't like that elsewhere and the icicles of fear began to form. The family heard about a Jew who underwent five hundred strokes of the rod for not attending Holy Communion; another was exiled to Siberia. Jews were being hanged for not attending or participating in Christian services. The Russian Church became increasingly harsh and vindictive. It became obvious that just to be Jewish was to be regarded as a criminal deserving punishment. Soon the secret police of the Tsar were mingling with the people of Bialystok and my family were considering taking the giant step of fleeing to the happy land, the promised land of America.

Any indecision was soon swept away by one word. It was a word which meant much the same as a sentence of life imprisonment. Conscription.

All the young men lived in terror of being conscripted into the

Tsar's army and the Zoltie brothers were no exceptions. They knew they risked the prospect of five years in the colours followed by thirteen in the militia, with the prospect of the army for life if they lacked the means of buying themselves out. The pay wasn't even worth considering, being, at the time, eight roubles a year. Of course you got your food but that consisted of black bread, boiled buckwheat and meat soup (or fish soup on fast days).

The option was to flee the country but that meant abandoning their hard-won business. It also meant leaving behind their parents who, although still fit and working, were both well into their sixties. The family was close. How were the brothers to leave their ageing and much-loved mother and father behind to face such a hopeless and dangerous future?

It was their parents, however, hardy and stoical, who made the final decision and ended their sons' confusion, if not their sorrow. Neither parent wanted to see their sons wasting their lives in the futile drudgery of the army, battling for a cause they'd all come to detest. The old folk had had their lives, and the young men must go off and make their own lives in an atmosphere of freedom and hope.

So it was that in 1900 the three brothers walked to Bialystok station, carrying what they could in small knapsack bundles. The first hurdle was to reach Danzig on the coast of the Baltic, a journey of some three hundred miles. From there, the distances were greater because they were unknown. Hyman had decided on America. He felt sure he could become rich in such a country. At first, Karl and my father favoured Britain. They imagined Victoria as a great empress ruling without oppression or hatred over a modern world of freedom and enterprise.

The whistle blew and the wheels began to turn. The carriages were packed with young people seeing their parents and families disappear for the last time, amid clouds of steam. And soon, loved ones and the town of Bialystok became no more than memories as the train thundered towards Warsaw. The brothers

7

were on their way to the coast. They sat silent, filled with the conflicting emotions of hope and grief.

They were also filled with insecurity. What they were doing was illegal and anywhere along the way they might be apprehended and taken for punishment. There was more fear in Warsaw. They were tense as they finally crossed the east Prussian border, but once in Danzig they felt free to talk openly about their plans. Karl the businessman, after careful thought, had changed his mind and decided to go to America with Hyman. This left my father to face his uncertain future alone, but he stuck to his choice of Britain and sorrowfully parted from his brothers for the last time.

It was dark when Maurice Zoltie stood on the deck of the ship leaving Danzig harbour. There would be no one waiting to welcome him when he arrived in England and he spoke not one word of the language. He turned to face the wind. He knew it would be a long night.

CHAPTER THREE

The Happy Land

The first thing Father required when he arrived in England was a job, so he made his way to Leeds where there already was a Jewish population. But perhaps Leeds was just too different from Bialystok; he couldn't settle. It seemed to him that the people were wholly motivated by business and profit. There was a harsh materialism which the warmth of his family hadn't prepared him for. His unease was such that he decided to move on. He travelled north to Edinburgh, capital of Scotland. But this time he wasn't alone. Leeds had given him the most important person in his life: the young woman who was to become my mother.

Her parents already lived in Edinburgh, so there was somewhere to stay when they got off the train, carrying their few possessions. The house was a tiny top flat in Arthur Street and conditions must have been impossibly cramped. My parents married in 1902 and, with considerable relief, moved into their own house, even though it was little more than a single rented room. There were thousands of people, Scots, Irish, Italians and Jews, living in similarly grim conditions. The high tenements had four or more landings, each of which led to a long, dimly-lit corridor. Any light came from a grimy, cracked cupola of sorts, set into the roof. Some of the buildings had tiny windows which let in small patches of daylight. At night, a gas jet would flicker and throw shadows on the walls and worn stone steps. Each landing had one toilet which might be shared, in some cases, by dozens of people. Chamber-pots would be brought out from the rooms in the mornings and emptied down the communal toilet. Someone would make sure there was always a supply of cut-up newspaper hanging on a wire or piece of string.

9

Some houses, like that of my parents, had their own stone sink and cold water supply. Less lucky people had to share a water supply out on their landing. Families would sleep, cook and eat in one room but, as usually happened, if the family grew in numbers, another room on the landing could be rented. My parents quickly produced four children, Reuben, Karl, Motty and Lena, and managed to exist in two rooms until 1913. Then, with the little money they'd managed to scrape together, they flitted to the comparative luxury of 15 St Leonard's Hill, a few minutes away. It was there that I was born on the nineteenth of May, 1914.

Though the house was an improvement, the family were still doing most of their shopping and socialising in the same area with the same people. The synagogue was the hub of their community and my parents would never have considered moving to another part of the city, even if they could have afforded to. Our Happy Land must have seemed like a self-imposed ghetto to the local Scots people.

The Jews did stick together but this was hardly unnatural. After centuries of persecution they had an innate knowledge that there was some hope of safety in numbers. In a way, the Richmond area was a kind of halfway house. Recently arrived emigrés could pick up the language and customs of their newly adopted land from the Jews who had already begun to blend with the local population. So my father, with difficulty, did his best to learn the unique Scottish Yiddish which was the language of The Happy Land. This wasn't such an odd language as outsiders might imagine it to be. Many words then in common use among the Scots were similar or identical to German, and so the Scots dialects blended easily with the German Yiddish of the immigrants. But to confuse matters at home, a relative in America used to send letters to St Leonard's Hill begging my parents to cross the Atlantic and join him; the letters were in Russian and had to be taken to the local baker for translation. Language problems were eased slightly by the fact that Mother, who herself had a Dutch mother and a German father, possessed a smattering of English.

The household inevitably was a poor one but the neighbours, both Jewish and Scottish, were also poor and so we never felt particularly deprived. Our home had the important qualities of warmth, love and laughter. It also had noise and smells. It was the noise which I, Hyman Zoltie, eventually grew to loathe.

Our house consisted of two rooms plus a large kitchen with a stone sink where everybody washed and an unlit lavatory. We were on the first floor of a grey stone tenement. At the front, we faced across the narrow street to another high row of houses; there were no gardens. We, however, had a considerable bonus. At the back, facing east, our kitchen window looked onto the back green where the women hung their washing. The ground there rose so steeply up to a rocky knoll that we had a view only from the top half of our window. But what a view it was! Beyond the flapping sheets and shirts, there stretched the magnificent panorama of what we called the King's Park, now Holyrood or the Queen's Park. We could see, from our kitchen sink, the high volcanic cliffs of Salisbury Crags. In the spring the steep slopes below them would dazzle us on sunny days with their vast stretches of bright yellow gorse flowers. And over to the right we could see Arthur's Seat, over eight hundred feet high, towering over the surrounding park and city. While most other people looked out onto the backs of other tenements, we were blessed with a view as good as any picture postcard.

Because of the unusual situation of our tenement, the families who lived below us actually had to climb up into the back green. The buildings there have long ago been swept away but, at the time of writing, the stone steps leading to the drying green still remain, surrounded by new young trees and half-overgrown by lush grass. When I was young, our street used to descend steeply in a northerly direction until its name changed to the Dumbie-dykes: this peculiar name arose from the fact that there was once a school for deaf and dumb children in the area.

My bedroom, like the kitchen, faced the back and also had a dramatic view across the park with its hills and valleys. But for some reason unknown to me, the window was never opened to let in any air. I say 'my' bedroom, but there were few people in our area who had the luxury of a room to themselves. In fact, my room was dominated by the presence of my older brothers, Reuben, Karl and Motty. For the first five years of my life I was consigned ignominiously to a cot. I outgrew it and protested, but there was nowhere else for me to go. Eventually, Reuben, being the biggest, got the luxury of a single bed to himself and I was deposited in the same bed as Karl and Motty. At first, I slept between my two brothers, but as I got bigger I was put to the bottom of the bed where I attempted to sleep, engulfed as I was, in the unforgettable odours of my brothers' feet. Through the long nights Motty and Karl fought an endless battle for possession of the bedclothes. No matter who won, I was generally left exposed to the draughts. Sometimes, in desperation, I settled for the floor. At least the air was slightly fresher.

I suppose the limited washing facilities also contributed to the fact that I can remember the pervasive smell of bodies. The atmosphere was, in a way, quite comforting. It seemed to mark out our territory, where we belonged. A pleasanter atmosphere, thankfully, permeated through our house a great deal of the time: that was the daily aroma of Mother's cooking. It was easy to forget the bedroom *and* the lavatory when she was busy preparing a savoury chicken or fruit dessert.

The second bedroom of the house faced onto the street. The buildings opposite meant that it was always in gloom, even if we cleaned and polished the window. The bright floral wallpaper didn't seem to help much either. This was, initially, my parents' room. We called it the dining-room but it was so full of furniture that we always ate, like most of other families, in the warmth of the kitchen. As well as my parents' bed, the so-called dining-room also had to accommodate two other beds, two big dusty moquette arm chairs, an expansive table, a wooden cupboard and six dining-room chairs. As the family expanded and Jack, Sydney, Anna, Ella and Betty appeared on the overcrowded scene, my parents took refuge in the kitchen where they slept in the recess, behind a curtain. This meant they were in a good position to catch any member of their tribe who might try to sneak through in the night, to pinch a cake or a biscuit. A memory which remains with me is of the six dining-room chairs which seemed to be eternally carried back and forward between the front room and the kitchen, according to the dictates of people present.

Life was centred in the kitchen. At first, the cooking was done on an old-fashioned grate with an oven, heated by coal. Then we managed to get a basic gas cooker. The rooms were all lit by gas and a common errand was to be sent out to the drysalter to buy a new mantle for one of the lights. The sink had one tap which was brass with a worn wooden handle. A huge blackened kettle was permanently just off the boil, until it was time again for tea. It stood at the side of the grate. All our floors were covered in cold linoleum with the occasional rug or piece of carpet here and there. There was a big folding table in the kitchen but the family rarely ate all together as we tended to arrive home at different times. Mother had to organise a kind of running buffet service throughout the day until my father arrived home, often around nine at night.

Despite our lack of 'mod cons', Mother insisted on regular bath nights, taking up whole evenings, when the big metal bath would be dragged out and placed in front of the blazing coal fire. We would line up to be stood, one by one, in the steaming tub and scrubbed mercilessly by Mother. The youngest went first and the eldest last. I remember one occasion when my sister Lena, obviously bored with the waiting, decided on a little experiment. She'd clearly been watching Motty's bare bottom with some interest and was wondering how it would react to a quick prod from the red-hot poker. Motty, naked and howling, almost bounced off the ceiling in agony and Lena was banished forthwith to bed in deep disgrace.

We may have lacked the luxury of a proper bathroom but we did, at least, have the luxury of our own lavatory. It was tiny and, though there was a stub of candle in a makeshift holder, we invariably forgot to take matches with us and had to sit or stand in the dark. There was a small window which could open into the common stair but, fortunately for our neighbours, it was always kept tightly closed.

Our mornings were pandemonium. Everybody wanted to use the lavatory at the same time and the innocent occupier would be subjected to torrents of angry abuse. As the door had no lock, there was no chance of the smelly cubby-hole becoming a place of quiet contemplation. My brothers thought nothing of wrenching it open and revealing me to the world in all my indignity. I once got so tired of this that I tied my braces, still attached to the front of my trousers, to the door handle. I sat down in the vain hope of a few precious minutes of undisturbed tranquillity. However, one of my brothers yanked open the door with such sudden ferocity that I was all but catapulted across the lobby, through the bedroom and out the window. I loved my family but I couldn't help feeling at times that there was just no escape from the endless proximity of people in that house.

The lobby, or hall, was the only other space in the house, but it was always dark unless a door was left open. A big coal bunker, which was usually about two-thirds full of dross, occupied part of the lobby. There was also a grandfather clock which seemed huge to me; it was always too fast or too slow. Its lack of precision seemed appropriate to our chaotic lives.

The one person who missed most of the chaos of the mornings was Father. He rose at six on weekdays to go to work. Lying awake at the feet of Karl and Motty, I would listen to him, busy at the black range in the kitchen. I would hear him impatiently rattling the poker through the iron ribs at the front. I could picture the clouds of white ash dust rising, and imagine the hot, dry smell of it. Then would come the sharp cracking of the firewood as the flames caught, and our fire would be lit for another day.

I could imagine him straightening his back as he let out a cry of 'Oi-yoi-foof!' Then came the sound of the gushing tap and the groaning pipe as he splashed himself awake at the sink. He did this, as he did most of his daily tasks, with a kind of ferocious enthusiasm.

By the time he left he would be dressed in his thick Scottish tweeds, chosen for the protection they gave him against the Scottish climate. He wore signet rings and in his waistcoat pocket he carried his most prized possession, a gold watch – with a guarantee. A final touch of style was the decorous chain which hung, attached to the watch, in the fashion popularised by the late Prince Albert.

My father's life as a travelling man was tough, and we were lucky he was so strong. He had an inherent desire to be his own boss and provide for his own family. Having had the tobacconist's shop in Bialystok, I don't think he could have put up with working for someone else. And though the Scots were tolerant towards us, in hard times they would naturally employ a Scot before a Jew. So my father continued on his idiosyncratic way, devising all manner of schemes and projects to make a living. Free enterprise was his way of surviving and he seemed to thrive on it; he was a true entrepreneur. Almost from the moment he arrived in Edinburgh, he bought wholesale anything he could and tramped the streets trying to sell his wares for a small profit. As his horizons broadened and he ventured further afield, he never missed a chance to try to sell something. Tram conductors and ticket collectors at railway stations were, to Father, all potential customers. Buying and selling occupied his whole working life in Scotland. He had no time for such time-wasting inconveniences as receipts, income-tax returns or any kind of paperwork, and inevitably his financial affairs would get into a terrible muddle. His approach to business was simple and straightforward and he never really came to terms with the more complex ways of the twentieth century.

Old Joe the Jew, as he came to be known, never faltered from the strict faith of his upbringing; the ancient faith seemed to lend him added strength. He was also a teetotaller. He expected high standards of behaviour from his sons and daughters and did his utmost to bring us up in strict conformity.

His life in Poland also seemed to have left him with a certain inner strength. Some of his business projects here were doomed to be failures but he never seemed to despair. He would be up again at dawn, preparing the fire, ready to start all over again.

CHAPTER FOUR

Our Tribe

There were so many strong, loud personalities in our St Leonard's Hill home that they must have left their mark on me. In retrospect, I see myself, little Hymie, as the shyest and perhaps the most introverted member of the household. I was the child who tended to get dominated by the others.

Reuben had an important position in the family, being the eldest son. He was of smallish build with an unusually straight nose. We used to joke that he could be mistaken for a goy (a Gentile). Karl was perhaps the least sophisticated of our tribe. Some people thought him slightly simple and, certainly, his habit of sucking his finger didn't help matters. Motty was son number three. Nowadays he would probably be described as 'streetwise'. He was tough and fast-talking and something of a rebel. If Motty thought he could get away with taking advantage of someone, he rarely hesitated. I was next in line, with my feelings of claustrophobia, ever aware of being hemmed in by walls of people, and noise. I was also, despite the size of the family, a lonely child. I was even born in a very unfortunate year – 1914. (Father volunteered for military service when war broke out but was rejected because of his flat feet.) We were a varied bunch and Jack was serious and studious with academic leanings. Sydney was the last son to be born; he had a shrewd brain and considerable musical ability. He played the guitar and I remember him singing folk songs in the house.

My parents also found time to produce four daughters. The oldest was Lena; she was a tall, skinny girl with an unusual, high-pitched voice. She fancied herself as a singer, the rest of us weren't so sure. Anna was lively and full of fun while Ella was the opposite, quiet and reserved. Betty was the youngest girl and always something of a mystery. She had frizzy hair and big, brown, spaniel-like eyes. When she was older, she would stay out very late, in spite of Father's threats to lock her out of the house. Sometimes at two or three in the morning, one of us would hear her stealthy knock at the door and creep into the lobby to let her in.

But despite all the seething life of my brothers and sisters, it was Father who was the dominant figure. I suppose he'd brought with him the habits of a much wilder time and place. He was the one who would wield the leather belt. In some ways he was like a coiled spring and we had to tread warily in his presence. An instinct for survival had contributed to his fierceness and tension. He tended to regard us as more like assistants than children. His business enterprises were often put before our education. It was left to Mother to provide us with warmth and comfort.

Occasionally Father would pause long enough to speak to us and tell us something of his past. It seemed a strange, alien world to us, living as we did in that grey Scottish street. I would watch him inhaling his cigarette deeply and imagine him back in Bialystok, rolling the aromatic tobacco leaves in the dark back of his shop. These shared moments were unusual, however. I tend more to recall the restless man with a relentless drive, a man who, at times, would make impossible demands on his young family and who would reduce me to an outburst of tears. Unfortunately, Father had no time for tears.

I don't want to idealise my mother but inevitably, in contrast with Father, she seemed a welcome harbour in which to escape the storms. Her background was more urbane, her manner smoother. I associate her with quiet dignity, and love. It seems a miracle to me that she managed to control her ranting, ravenous brood and cope with all the cooking, baking, bathing, washing, ironing, sweeping, nursing and even her reading. She did it all without any sense of panic or rush. Just a quiet, steady rhythm, which was a source of comfort to me.

As in any Jewish household, food was of prime importance.

We always had enough, though at times there seemed to be a lack of variety. There were the chickens and, of course, the eggs. The birds turned up at the table, meal after meal, but Mother, rather like an alchemist, succeeded in transforming them into all manner of magical dishes. A special occasion would be the appearance of her marvellous borsch soup, made from beetroots. She used an old Eastern European recipe and I can still recall the taste today. Like the Scots, we would treat ourselves to rich smoky kippers on a Sunday morning, followed by toast, jam and tea. The meals were always important, but even more so at the weekends when the whole straggling family had a chance to sit down peaceably together.

Like my brothers and sisters, I had to take my share of going to the shops – or going the messages, as we say in Edinburgh. As I've mentioned, the chickens were my particular duty: I had to get them ritually slaughtered. Sometimes even the rabbi (or the rabbie, as some Scots called him) got involved with chickens. Our dietary laws were strict and, if there was any doubt about a bird, the rabbi was the ultimate authority. Sometimes he would have to check to see what a bird had been eating and this could lead to its being condemned as unfit for consumption. A bird with cancer would be rejected; a Scottish housewife might just use the same bird, not being trained to recognise that anything was amiss. To outsiders, the Jewish dietary laws can seem finicky and old-fashioned but they are, in fact, eminently sensible, having been originally inspired by a concern for hygiene. Jews regard life as a gift from God and that gift has to be protected; hence the strict rules about food, all geared towards self-preservation. With chickens and other animals, we were supposed to know where they'd been in the weeks prior to their slaughter.

I used to carry the chickens along Beaumont Place and into the busier St Leonard's Street, where our nearest kosher butcher was situated. There were several Jewish shops in St Leonard's Street, including a tailor and a cobbler, though this was, strictly speaking, just outside The Happy Land area. The best known baker was Kleinberg's in East Crosscauseway. This shop, at the time of writing, was still producing delicious kosher bread. It was run by the Kleinberg family until as recently as the mid 1980s.

I suppose the shops that we used were often overcrowded and unhygienic places in those days before food became subject to a host of rules and regulations. There were two dairies close to our house and I would be sent out to collect our milk. I took along a tin with a lid on it. The large churns would be lined up along the wall, and pint or half-pint ladles would be used to measure out the creamy liquid into my tin. I've heard that special kosher milk could be obtained from a farm at Gilmerton, to the south of Edinburgh, but I'm not wholly certain about that. All our milk was, of course, unpasteurised. Butter was cut from a huge block, patted into shape with two wooden spatulas, then wrapped in greased paper.

Our whole area was grossly overcrowded, with the high tenements housing many people per room. This meant that there were plenty of customers for a concentration of shops of every kind. The two dairies I mentioned were separated by only about a hundred yards, yet both did good business. I remember that it was common for shopkeepers to live in one or two rooms at the back of their shops, often with a sizeable family. The shops all had distinctive smells, since most of the goods – cheese, tea, tobacco or whatever – were sold loose and measured out. We never dreamt of buying anything in a tin. A result of this manner of selling was that all the shops seemed to me, as a little boy, to be filled with scales. They intrigued me with their jangling metallic parts and sturdy brass weights. It would have been worth becoming a shopkeeper just to get to use those magical scales.

Though the people around us were often poor, I believe they used to get enough to eat because it was easier then than nowadays to eat cheaply. Scraps could be bought from the butcher's for next to nothing, so there was hardly a family, Jewish or Scottish, which didn't have a pot of broth permanently simmering.

One of our favourites was, naturally, chicken soup which Mother could make deliciously with herbs. Vegetables could be bought very cheaply in mixed bags. I would collect them from a shop in Carnegie Street which also did good business by selling soft fruit at half price. A regular sight could be seen early in the morning outside Young Brothers, the bakers in The Pleasance. Bread, and what we called teabread, from the previous day was sold off cheaply and there would always be a queue of mothers and children waiting for a very necessary bargain. It wasn't unusual to collect a supply of the stuff in a pillow-case. As the bread wasn't fresh, toast was a great favourite but this had to be made by holding a slice of bread on the end of a knife in front of the glowing grate. It was a long, slow process which led, inevitably, to much impatience around the breakfast table.

We rarely had newspapers at home. As children, we had no interest in affairs outside our immediate world. I can't imagine either of my parents having the time to read newspapers and perhaps their inevitably limited command of English made it a waste of money to buy them. I occasionally got a comic called *Comic Cuts* but it didn't come into the house regularly. At the newsagent's I would be fascinated by the cover of the *Police Gazette* with its lurid illustrations of terrible crimes; it was a popular magazine at the time. Betting on the horses was popular, too. Men who had very little would risk money they couldn't afford in the vain hope of instant riches. This meant that the newsagent always had a good stock of *Racing Gazette* and *Sporting Times*. *Sexton Blake* detective magazines were usually on display and, for the women, I remember *My Weekly* and *Peg's Paper*. Nearly every man seemed to smoke when I was a boy and I often stood in the queue, being ignored, as men came in for their ten Woodbines, Capstan or Gold Flake. Some of the immigrants preferred the stronger Turkish Pashas. Like most of the shops, the newsagent's was very close by, being further up St Leonard's Hill in a southerly direction. That same stretch of buildings still contains a little pub called Jeanie Deans Tryste. It was there at 67 St Leonard's Hill when I was a boy and, as I write, it is still operating, although surrounded by waste land and rubble. The area was awash with pubs, all very basic in the Scottish fashion of the time. They meant little to me, however, as my parents never drank anything except the tiny amounts of sweet Palestine wine which formed a part of our religious observances.

My favourite shop was the confectioner's in Carnegie Street. The bargain there was broken biscuits. There were large square tins full of them and a good bagful cost very little indeed. I hardly ever saw a whole biscuit, unless it was baked by my Mother. On a hot summer afternoon a favourite treat was a dark, sweet and fizzy drink called Vantas. This was poured from a tank and the bubbles were added by a cylinder of carbon dioxide attached to the side of the tank. I wouldn't be surprised if a few young teeth were sacrificed as a result of addiction to that particular beverage. If I ever had a penny to spend I would run round to Carnegie Street and try to make the impossible choice among the dolly mixtures, sherbet dabs, liquorice sticks, Nelson's striped mint balls and lollipops in more colours than the rainbow. For young gamblers, an added attraction at the sweetie shop was the lucky dip. You paid a ha'penny and rummaged around in a bin until your fingers closed on something hard and tightly-wrapped in coloured paper. If you were lucky you pulled out a new silver threepenny bit; there were only a few in the bin. Usually, however, you had to settle for a sweet or small novelty.

At that time, around 1920, no one in the area had electricity or even gas heating. Everybody relied on the coalman, who was a weekly visitor in the street, with his horse and cart. There was a huge coalyard just up the street and there was a special track, known as the Innocent Railway, to bring coal into the city centre from Dalkeith. I've heard that it wasn't unusual for men in our area, when times were hard, to sneak into the St Leonard's Coal Depot and fill a bag with coal. It was absolutely necessary for the heating and cooking in many houses where there was no gas cooker or ring.

We found the arrival of the coal a great event, but Mother must have hated the weekly disruption. I can't remember the year but I do remember the coalman shouting, 'Best coal! 1/6d a bag!' That was 7½p for a hundredweight. He came to our street on Wednesday mornings and all the housewives could be seen dodging back and forward to their front windows. Then the horse's hooves would clip-clop on the cobbles and there would be much frantic signalling and calling up and down as everyone gave their orders, one, two or even three bags. Then, clothed in his leather apron and dusty cap, and black from his damp fore-head to the soles of his boots, the coalman would climb the stairs and stamp into our lobby. He seemed to me, as he puffed under his lumpy, grimy load, more powerful than any circus strongman. There would be a brief pause as he halted at our bunker, then house and stair would resound with a noise like the most terrible thunderstorm as the black lumps crashed out of the sack. Dark, choking dust would rise like steam, engulf the poor old grand-father clock then belch out into the stair. Mother was always nearby to make sure she hadn't been given more than her fair share of dross. The coins would be dropped into a black palm and the coalman would be gone for another week. Mother would have to clean up the lobby while someone, one of my brothers perhaps, got the job of breaking up the bigger lumps with a hatchet.

In discussing our food and shopping arrangements, I haven't yet mentioned the buying of fish. Leith, Granton and Newhaven were all only a couple of tram rides away from us and, at the time, were thriving fishing harbours and markets. Good fresh fish was readily available from shops, stalls and barrows, and fishwives in traditional costumes would sell cockles, mussels, whelks and winkles outside the pubs. Fish was popular with all families as it was, then, much cheaper than meat. The cheapest fish of all, though we didn't buy it, was a dried fish – cod I think – like a big, stiff board. It had to be soaked overnight but provided a nourishing meal for an extremely low cost. Our own methods of obtaining fish, however, were sometimes more complicated than a mere visit to a shop.

The green expanse of the King's Park, in contrast to our narrow streets, was like the open countryside to us. A couple of minutes from our stair entrance, we would climb the wide stone steps at Heriot Mount and enter a playground which would be the envy of any city child. There were steep hills to climb and the ruins of an old chapel to play in. But there was also the irresistible attraction of three lochs, St Margaret's, Dunsapie and Duddingston. My brother Motty decided that he would take up angling. It wasn't because he was interested in gazing all day long into the rippling waters of Duddingston Loch; he thought he'd discovered a quick and easy way to make some money. Fishing was a popular local hobby and it was quite common for men or boys to arrive at our door with fish for sale. Mother was usually happy to buy, as were many of the other Jewish housewives. It was usually pike which she bought. It was very bony and not in great demand so, I presume, it made a cheap meal. By the time Mother had finished cooking it, there was, somehow, never a bone to be found.

Motty made up his mind to enter the market and used to take me along on his fishing expeditions. He couldn't afford the luxury of a fancy rod but bought a fishing line with a hook. Filled with anticipation, we scrabbled and poked around in the back-green until we had enough worms to use as bait. On our first day, Motty caught one fish and I could see he was restless and dis-appointed. Things were moving far too slowly for him so he approached the other anglers and talked them into selling part of their catch – for very low prices. Soon, he gave up the hook and line altogether and just went to the loch with his basket late in the day and bought his 'catch'.

He ran into trouble when he tried to sell his fish to Mother at inflated prices. She was far too shrewd for him and, besides, she could still get her supplies cheaply from her regular callers. She didn't need her son to act as a middle-man. Motty soon realised that he wasn't going to get rich quick by dealing in fish. His basket soon joined the hook and line in a cupboard, gathering dust.

The fishermen and the coalman were only a few of our regular callers at St Leonard's Hill. Almost every day there seemed to be someone beating at the heavy front door. They soon learned to pull the clanging brass bell if they wanted an answer as Mother was slightly hard of hearing. We were usually short of money but Mother, like many of the women in the district, found it impossible to turn away hawkers or beggars. She wouldn't keep people standing on the dark stair but invariably asked them into the house. If a tramp came asking for hot water, she would make him a pot of tea. Salesmen would spread out their trinkets and bric-a-brac and Mother, feeling sorry for them, would always buy something, however useless. This would make Father angry: he would arrive home late after a long day's selling and tell her he could have got whatever she'd bought much more cheaply from his wholesaler. Unlike Father, Mother hated to bargain and always paid a salesman the price he asked. She trusted total strangers and would leave them alone in the front room while she went to the kitchen to make tea. She was, however, sensible enough always to keep her purse in the pocket of her apron. She gave money readily to charity collectors, tinkers and gipsies but I don't think Father ever knew about that. Like most working-class women in Scotland, she controlled the housekeeping budget and Father was happy to let her get on with it.

I heard that the gipsies had a good method of collecting money. Young women, often with babies, would occasionally call at the door and be given something by Mother. I was told later that they used to leave a secret mark somewhere at the bottom of the tenement stair where they knew someone kind or charitable lived. This acted as a guide to other gipsies who came along to beg.

I didn't know of anyone in our area who owned their own home. Since all the rooms and houses were rented, another caller each week would be the rent man. Mother had to make sure there was always enough kept aside to pay him. Rents then, of course, were measured in shillings rather than pounds.

As a boy, I grew to see my mother as the one who gave, and my father as the one who made demands. In my young mind they came to seem like opposites, two extremes with me in the middle. Another problem, one which touched every Jewish child growing up in or near The Happy Land, was that of nationality. All around us were the Scots but our parents regarded them as goys, outsiders we were not encouraged to mix with. My father wanted to keep us well inside the orthodox tradition and, dutifully, I would refrain from mixing with the Scottish children. But it was quite impossible for me to ignore the Scots. Scotland was the only country I knew. Father had his own, very different, roots.

The Scots attracted me. They seemed cool and restrained, with a certain quiet strength. I think it was their comparative quietness that appealed to me the most. At home it was colourful and sometimes crazy; life pulsated and, as I've said, it was always noisy. I craved some of that quietness which I came to associate, rightly or wrongly, with the Scots.

The only time I got to mix socially with Scottish children was when Father, a staunch Freemason of the Solomon Lodge in Duncan Street, took us to his annual party where there was a wondrous array of balloons, crackers, trifles, cakes and sweeties. Here I discovered Father Christmas but also encountered, for the first time, the friendliness of the Edinburgh people. I'm sure it was these parties, with their Christian associations, which started me on my journey away from my Jewishness and from my father's beliefs. It seems ironic, looking back now, that it was Father who so happily took me along.

CHAPTER FIVE

Our Orthodoxy

In later years my father was saddened by the fact that none of his sons and daughters grew up to share his orthodox beliefs. As children, our lives were inextricably interwoven with the religious rituals and events of our ancestors but, like children anywhere, we found much of it of limited interest. We were more concerned with what was happening outside in the street or at the local cinema. We managed to avoid a fair amount of our early morning prayers as Father would often be away to work before we emerged from our beds. If Father was still around, we made a great display of putting on our black caps and praying loudly. But this was only while he was in the bedroom watching us. We would stop when he went to the kitchen but one of his loud shouts was enough to get us reciting again at full pitch. However, we used to skip pages here and there. I never heard God complain.

The customs and rituals were all-important to Father. For him, it was an end in itself to be a good and pious Jew attending the synagogue regularly. He made us wear our fringed shawls for morning prayers but we paid little heed to the significance of the garments. Strict Jews wore a four-cornered fringed undershirt during the day; we never did. Another ritual which we couldn't take seriously was the ceremonial dedicating of arm and brain to God. This involved taking two small black leather boxes containing scrolls (phylacteries), and tying one to the forehead and one to the left bicep. We found it an embarrassing nuisance and laughed at it.

A typical prayer session with the young Zolties would involve solemn snatches of scripture such as, 'Now, therefore, if you will truly obey My voice', 'Keep My covenant' and 'You shall be a nation of priests' interrupted by more earthly cries of, 'Stop kickin' me, you fool', 'A didnae touch ye' and 'Are ye goin' up tae the park for a game?' Such undisciplined devotion inevitably led Father to intervene in a futile attempt at rounding up his errant flock and chasing it back into the orthodox fold.

We often found these morning prayers a trial and of course we would be worried about getting away in time for school. Friday nights, however, were different. Then, there was strict observance of all the formalities and I, for one, welcomed the peaceful atmosphere which descended on our household as the candles were lit and the plaited bread was made ready for our return from the synagogue.

In Edinburgh we had an unusual arrangement of synagogues. There are many different types and sects of Jews around the world; in Edinburgh, even though there were only about four hundred Jewish families in all, there were also serious divisions. I can remember there being a very strict group of largely Eastern European Jews who became known locally as the Bolshies. They had their own separate synagogue in, if I remember correctly, Roxburgh Place. We went to an old draughty building which had previously been a Christian church. Our synagogue was known as the Central Shul and was at the point where Roxburgh Place, West Adam Street and Richmond Place met. There was a third synagogue, situated some distance away from The Happy Land, just off Lauriston Place and near Edinburgh College of Art. This was known as the Graham Street Shul and the Jews who went there were the ones who spoke most English and had become more assimilated into Scottish life. They tended to be better off financially than the families who worshipped at our Central Shul. Eventually, all the factions were brought together, in body at least, in 1932 when Rabbi Daiches took over the new big synagogue which is still in use in Salisbury Road.

By the time Saturday, our Sabbath, arrived we young ones were getting a little restless and dying to be out and about and doing things. Our activities were strictly curtailed, however –

much more so than those of the Scottish children on Sundays. Father would let us away with nothing. We couldn't light the fire or the gas or even carry a penny in our pockets. This meant that we had to have a Christian woman come in on Saturdays to perform a few necessary chores for us. Mind you, I expect that Mother got a few hours of welcome rest. The woman who helped us was called Peggy. She was glad of the money as her husband had a drink problem.

First thing on Saturday mornings, Peggy could be heard bustling around in the cold kitchen. The fire would be lit and the tea made. As this went on, my parents remained mysteriously out of sight in their bed in the recess, screened by a heavy curtain. Eventually, Peggy would give us all breakfast then return to give us our midday meal. She wasn't paid much but she ate with us and seemed to appreciate it. She would leave a gas-ring burning very low, so we would have a supply of hot water. It seemed strange to me then that the Law allowed us to fill a kettle but not light a gas-ring. I could remember nothing in any of our readings of the scriptures which referred to kettles and gas-rings. But, as I discovered, there *was* a law which stated that we must not kindle a fire. In later years, when houses began to get electricity, things were made much easier as it was generally agreed that to switch on an electric fire would not be contravening the Law; it wasn't actually kindling a fire.

Apart from our daily prayers and regular weekly rituals, we were expected to participate in all the other special occasions and festivals of the Jewish year. One of the better ones, as far as I was concerned, was Chanukah. It occurred around the same time as Christmas which, of course, was ignored by Father. I may have been unaware of the whole significance of Chanukah but I enjoyed the cakes and happy atmosphere. I remember we were touched on the head with a handkerchief containing silver threepennies. Once the ceremony was over, the coins were distributed among the children. That suited me. Our New Year was celebrated in September and that was just one more reason why it was difficult for me to blend with the Scottish children at school. I always seemed to be out of step with them and doing things at different times, in different ways. The Scottish New Year or Hogmanay was a huge celebration, more important than Christmas even, but as it invariably involved a fair amount of drinking and merry-making, my parents had nothing to do with it.

The Jews' most solemn time is the Day of Atonement or Yom Kippur. It was a fast day for us, and Mother and Father did their best to instil us with a suitable amount of reverence. We were expected to stay in the synagogue from nine in the morning until seven in the evening. That was a tall order for a gang of restless youngsters and we used to dread the long ordeal. One hour's relief for fresh air was allowed during the day.

On one occasion my brother Motty, always the rebel, decided that we should have a break from the rigorous fasting. When our time for fresh air arrived he took us all the way to a café in Corstorphine, in the west of Edinburgh. His theory was that we could have something there to eat and drink and, being so far away from The Happy Land, no one would know. When we got there we were considerably dumbfounded to find the place full of Jews, all eating and drinking, thinking they wouldn't be discovered. The café owner told us she always had lots of Jewish customers on fast days. It gave us a good laugh but also it was a fair indication of how the old ways were dying out as we all began to live more like the Scots who surrounded us.

It used to be a Scottish custom to hold a wake after someone died and, interestingly, we Jews had a similar custom. Prayers were said at the house of the deceased, so long as there was the requisite number of people present. Neighbours might come in to make up the numbers and one of the many practices was that, after a death, someone had to sit up with the body all night before the funeral. I recall when my grandfather died and Motty was selected for the vigil. Being a tough, no-nonsense kind of a chap, he seemed the best choice for the job. He managed to look unconcerned at the prospect before him, but was in fact terrified. I know because he told us about it later. He had been tense and had jumped every time one of the old floorboards creaked. His imagination had taken flight as the dark night wore on. At about three o'clock in the morning he'd been totally convinced that the coffin lid was beginning to move. Motty had sat, petrified, half expecting grandfather's withered hand to appear, and then. . . . Terrified as he was, Motty completed his vigil alone and we had to admire his courage.

These were times when death was dealt with by the family, with the help of the rabbi. Nowadays it seems institutionalised and can be made remote by hospitals and undertakers. Another important change is that people like my parents had their religious faith to support them at times of loss whereas I, like many others, lost my faith and any consolations it might have brought. My lifetime has seen many drastic changes, including the difference in society's attitude to death.

But, back in St Leonard's Hill, a day was not allowed to go by without us being reminded of our Jewishness. I remember vividly the fire and brimstone speeches of the rabbi. His arms would wave as he thundered down a holocaust of words on his trembling congregation and berated them for their sins. A festival which has lodged itself particularly in my memory is the Passover. This is partly because Father always seemed to find the money from somewhere to have new suits made for us. We felt proud and smart but new clothes were so unusual that I remember sitting in the synagogue as stiffly as though my suit had been cut out of cardboard.

Even without the distraction of new clothes, it wasn't easy for us to follow what was happening in the synagogue. I could imagine a young Christian boy or girl losing interest at a church service, but we had the added problem of having our services conducted in Hebrew. We rarely knew what page we were supposed to be on, and sometimes our seniors would have to direct us to the correct page and line during the service. To help

31

us cope with the routine of the services and learn the Hebrew language, we were sent to special classes after our ordinary school was finished. This, of course, was something else which set us apart from the non-Jewish community. Other children would be playing hide and seek or football in the streets.

Looking back, it seems now that we Jewish children must have had very little time for fun and games. For most of the day I was at St Leonard's Primary School, just up the road. There were few Jewish children there, as it was situated beyond The Happy Land area. This made me feel like an outsider and matters were made worse by a bully who would wait at the gates to torment me when school was finished. I would escape his clutches, then run home for a bite to eat before setting out for Sciennes School, to the south of The Meadows. The classes there started about four o'clock and lasted an hour. We knew the Hebrew School as 'the cheder'. When it was over we had our other homework to do. We may not have been any brighter than the Scottish children but we were certainly made to use what mental abilities we had and I think the early training benefited us in later life.

My instructor at the cheder was the rabbi's assistant, and he had to be paid. I found this odd as I didn't have to pay for my ordinary lessons at St Leonard's, so when Father gave me the fees I decided the most sensible course was for me to keep this money for myself. Who would know? I rarely had any cash of my own, so it was exciting to have some coins buried in my pockets. I sat through the stories about Moses and Solomon but I didn't really want to hear all that ancient stuff. I was too busy thinking about the good times I would have, after cheder, with my new-found source of income. I was delighted with my own cleverness. I wasn't clever enough, however, to anticipate that the rabbi's assistant would wonder where his fees were and would go to the rabbi, who in turn would tackle my father who, in his turn, would reach for his leather strap and apply it loudly across my bare buttocks. When Father's temper got the better of him he displayed an absence of mercy more suited to the pages of the Old

Testament than twentieth century Scotland. This story suggests that, even as a boy, I had a nose for making money; but I was also learning that there were wrong as well as right methods of doing it.

The ways of our religion inevitably caused puzzlement to the non-Jews we encountered. The Scots found our custom of having separate plates for milk and meat dishes extremely odd. And at school, I could never have school dinners as they were unkosher. I always had to have my own sandwiches, specially prepared by Mother.

Father often travelled to Fife with his packs and did so across the old Forth Bridge, by train from Edinburgh's Waverley Station. Since a Jew has to say his prayers before he eats, Father often wouldn't have time for breakfast before leaving the house. Sometimes he would congregate with other Jewish traders in a compartment and have an impromptu prayer session. Occasionally, when I was old enough, he took me with him. I can remember one morning when a Scotsman rushed to catch the train and threw himself into our compartment at the last moment. He was startled to find it full of men wearing black skullcaps and fringed shawls, all chanting away in an unknown tongue. 'Excuse me,' the traveller inquired nervously, 'but is this the right train for Dundee?' The praying was interrupted by a few nods and he uneasily slid into a corner seat, perhaps wondering if he'd stumbled upon an occult sect travelling to a meeting in Fife.

When the prayers were completed and the train was steaming towards the Firth of Forth, the Scotsman was offered a share of breakfast, bread and salami. He nibbled nervously, obviously still unsure of his travelling companions. Father asked him what he did for a living, probably hoping eventually to sell him a watch or a ring before they reached their destinations. It turned out that he was a travelling salesman dealing in farm foodstuffs. Soon everyone was swapping selling stories, united by a common bond. The Scot relaxed and ate his bread and sausage contentedly.

The story amused my father and he liked to retell it; but sometimes, I think, it brought home to me the fact that religion, though usually regarded as a force for good, can be a divisive thing. I came to realise eventually that a strict adherence to the orthodox ways could not be part of *my* way forward, living in a Christian country in the twentieth century. But that was something my father could never understand.

All the same, I still have my good memories of our Friday evenings at home, after we'd been to the synagogue. We rarely saw Father all week but he was always back from his travels early on Fridays. We all ate together and there would be readings from the Jewish Bible. The tranquillity was bliss after a week of squabbling and shouting which sometimes got so bad that I wanted to pull a blanket over my head. On Friday evenings, even a slightly flippant comment by anyone would immediately be shushed by Father. I grew to love that atmosphere of calm.

CHAPTER SIX

Hens, Hymns, Ham and More Hens

The area where I was brought up is very different today. Slum clearance has made it unrecognisable and even the layout of some of the original streets has gone. North Richmond Street is now no more than a memory in the minds of some of Edinburgh's more senior citizens. Yet it was the thriving centre of The Happy Land when I was a boy. My fondest memory of the street is the Abbey cinema, where I would spend hours in the thick, smoky atmosphere, watching my screen heroes. All the local cinemas seemed to have a strong and musty smell which I can still recall. Was it disinfectant, furniture polish or just years of dust? Or all three? I don't know, but I can't watch an old film of Tom Mix or Pearl White on TV without that smell seeming to pervade the room.

In the 1920s and 1930s many Edinburgh people went to the cinema two or three times a week. I went as often as I could afford to, which was not as often as I would have liked. We called the Abbey our local flea-pit and I'm sure our description was pretty accurate. It wasn't unusual for me to be scratching franti cally before I got back to St Leonard's Hill. The Abbey, oddly enough, had taken over the site of one of Edinburgh's earlier synagogues, but I always knew it as a cinema. Ideally situated, right opposite, was Bullen's fish and chip shop. This was a very unusual establishment at the time as Mr Bullen used oil instead of animal fat or dripping for frying. This meant that his food could be classed as kosher and eaten by Jews, though it was a treat I couldn't afford at the time.

One of my less pleasant memories is of the Tron cinema. I was happily lost in the film when I realised the man in the next seat was trying to unbutton my trousers. This puzzled rather than alarmed me but I quickly changed my seat. I never thought to tell anyone about it; perhaps because I was brought up to believe that adults were always right and their behaviour was not to be questioned.

Another old Edinburgh street which has been lost was East Richmond Street. It used to meet The Pleasance, opposite the top of Salisbury Street. There were a great many Jewish families in these streets as well as the steep Brown Street and Arthur Street which led down to the Dumbiedykes. South Richmond Street has been replaced by an area of pretty gardens. The last time I saw it the trees were blossoming and it looked very different from the high grey tenements of my youth. The hub of this area was our synagogue, the Central Shul, which has been replaced by an ugly grey office block, clashing with its surroundings. That's progress.

If, in the 1920s, people from the politer, more refined districts of Edinburgh happened to wander into North or East Richmond Street, they could see immediately that this was no ordinary part of the Scottish capital. The buildings were high and dark and the cobbled roadway perhaps gleamed after a shower brought by the cold east wind, but there the similarities with the rest of Edinburgh ceased. There was a strange vitality that seemed very different. The scene was not a Scottish one. There was much extrovert activity: arms flayed and hands were outstretched in a thousand dramatic gestures as banter was traded and newspapers were argued over. People yelled their strange greetings from one pavement to another while, filling the roadway, were salesmen, scholars, schemers, inventors, rogues and rabbis. There were westernised Jews, urbane and blasé in their adopted tweeds. And there were orthodox Jews, stiff and ancient-looking in their black gaberdine frockcoats, wide-brimmed hats and prayer locks. Darting among them were the fledglings of this strange community, eager and quick to learn, laughing and ready for all manner of mischief. I was one of that new generation, energetically acquiring anything that might be of use to me in my journey ahead and always prepared to discard the ballast of the old ways so lovingly preserved by my parents.

My picture of the busy Happy Land has remained with me along with the smells, and even the stinks – these were unforgettable. When I used to return from the butcher with my sack of dead chickens, Father would devote his energies to organising his whole tribe into a great chicken-plucking co-operative. One object of this was to provide cheap filling for the cushions and pillows which Mother used to sew. At one point, Father used to take the chickens, one at a time, and hold them close to the coal fire until all the feathers were singed. When I was very young, I used to believe he was trying to roast the birds in their jackets! But, of course, the singeing speeded up the plucking. It also produced a pungent odour which never seemed to clear away from our house. Before long, we'd be up to our elbows in feathers and we'd be sniffing and sneezing with feathers up our nostrils, and in our ears and hair. There'd be feathers inside our collars and feathers clinging to our sweaty brows and woolly jumpers. Even at night, I remember, a poorly-stitched pillow might split apart in the turmoil of our bed and, once again, we'd be buried in feathers.

Another scene which I recall, complete with smells, is the public wash-house. The atmosphere was heavy, moist and strangely sweet. Sometimes I went there with Mother, who pushed a pram filled with what seemed like bales of dirty washing tied up in sheets. There was little time for relaxation once we got there. I remember Mother perspiring over the hot boilers, breathing in the reek of soap, steam and gas. The outcome of all this effort was half a day's ironing to be done in front of the fire at home. This filled the house with the pleasant, comforting smell of dry, freshly-laundered clothing. Our wash-house stood at the point where Davie Street met Simon Square. The building is still there but nearly derelict.

We couldn't afford the luxury of umbrellas so another distinctive smell used to be our outdoor clothes, on wet days, hanging on every available hook and chair to dry. That was a rather stale, unpleasant smell.

Another thing which can't be forgotten is the unmistakable,

sweet-sour smell of leather soaking in water. This penetrating odour is rarely encountered nowadays, but it will always remind me of my mother's father. He was a cobbler and lived at the top of a high winding stair in one room in Arthur Street where he also practised his craft of making boots, shoes and slippers. (Nowadays he would undoubtedly be contravening many sections of the Health and Safety at Work Act.) I remember him as a very old man who wore spats. His bowler hat was never off his head. He didn't seem to have to move about; he just sat there cramped over his awl, with tacks gripped between his lips. I used to be sent to Arthur Street when the soles and heels of my boots began to wear out. I loved to sit, drinking tea and eating my grandmother's biscuits, as the old man cut the tough pieces of leather into perfect shapes.

All the boys wore boots. These were bought to last and certainly took a lot of punishment on the football field or cobbled streets. I found my boots too heavy and never liked wearing them. They had metal toe-caps as well as metal on the heels. My best outfit for special occasions was a little sailor suit with a kerchief. Nowadays the idea seems odd but then it was not an unusual 'get-up' for a boy.

Undoubtedly the best smells of all, came from Mother's kitchen. We would find the hot wafting aromas irresistible. Honey, currant and seed cakes had to be kept in a cupboard under lock and key to prevent us from immediately devouring them, tray after tray. The key to the forbidden cupboard had to be kept hidden and sometimes I would spend long periods trying to lay my hands on it.

The kitchen, being the warmest room in the house, was where our many visitors used to congregate. On a Sunday morning you could find the rabbi along with Father and a whole host of friends and business acquaintances. The blethering was a tumult which would have drowned out the din at the Tower of Babel. All this, of course, tended to emphasise our permanent lack of space. It was impossible to have a personal territory in such a hubbub.

Our world, in retrospect, seemed a very sociable place but it could also be tough. Often a Jew would arrive from the Continent with only the clothes he wore, and no contacts. He might be given a sack of sponges or some cheap wares and it would be up to him to get out and get selling. There was, of course, no Social Security, so while there were men like my father, usually managing to make ends meet, there were many others, poorer than peasants, in frayed and ill-fitting clothes. There were, too, successful Jews who made a point of parading their wealth in elegant silks and expensive worsted cloths. And, as I've suggested, these social divisions were reflected in the fact that we had three synagogues in Edinburgh when I was young.

While living in the centre of a city, my father never seemed to lose his deep affinity with the countryside. I assume that was why he spent so much of his working time tramping round farms and villages. At one point he gave up the trains and invested in a bicycle. He'd set out, proudly independent, with his pack in the early morning. He'd cycle to such places as Auchendinny, Howgate and Peebles, to the south of Edinburgh. He would also pedal out to West Linton or deep into the rolling farmlands of East Lothian. I can remember him, as I lay in bed, kissing my mother noisily then clattering off down the stair with the bike on one shoulder and his pack on the other.

Father's tireless endeavours ensured that there was, nearly always, plenty of food but, very occasionally, he couldn't make enough money. It was then that he would fall back on his talent for bartering. I remember once we were finding it difficult to get by; we'd even run out of chickens and eggs. Out in the street, Father happened to meet an imposing looking gentleman whom I'll just refer to as Sir Leon. Sir Leon had heard that Father was struggling and he wished to help. We were therefore invited along to a big hall and given a meal, free of charge. I'm sure this went against Father's pride but he was prepared to put up with it to make sure we ate.

We attended several of these meal sessions until, once, we were given a short talk. That was followed by what at first seemed like a cheery sing-song. 'Vos is das?' my father thundered. We looked at him in alarm. I thought he was in danger of exploding. The cheery song was the well-known hymn, *Jesus loves me*. Father had caught the one word 'Jesus' and rose to his feet. He rounded us all up and marched us into the street. That was the last of our free meals.

We learned that Sir Leon, although a Jew, had been converted to Christianity. The meetings were his attempts at gaining further converts. But he hadn't realised that Father would have us all face starvation rather than sing the praises of Jesus Christ.

The Salvation Army band used to play regularly at the end of our street. Father knew we liked to watch and listen but always warned us about going too close. He was afraid we'd hear the Christian preaching and our own beliefs would be contaminated.

My stories make Father seem like the stricter of my parents but Mother, although quieter, was deeply religious and quick to chastise any of us if she suspected backsliding. I remember a time when she had good reason to criticise Father. He hadn't been making much money as the farmers he'd been visiting were all experiencing hard times. One farmer badly needed clothes for his children but had absolutely no money to buy them from Father. The two men sat in the farmer's cottage, discussing what could be done. A smoked leg of ham hung from the rafters, and the farmer, as a joke, said he would exchange it for some clothes. He knew Father was Jewish and expected that the highly un-kosher ham would be regarded as worse than an abomination. But Father's business acumen began to war with his religious scruples. His religion forbade him to touch the meat but he knew how much the ham was worth. How could he get back to Edinburgh without actually touching it?

Then, as he often did, Father had a brainwave. Motty, my brother, had often been in trouble for ignoring his prayers and paying little heed to his religion. He was a perpetual thorn in

Father's orthodox flesh. But now Father could put Motty's lack of qualms to profitable use.

Father made a deal with the farmer then rushed back to Edinburgh, looking nervous and shifty as though he expected at any moment to be struck by a thunderbolt. A secret arrangement was made with Motty, and the ham, wrapped mysteriously in newspaper, was delivered by Motty to a local grocer. Father got his money and the farmer got new clothes for his children. Father reckoned he'd completed a successful bit of business. Until the following day.

Mother happened to go to the grocer in question and he, unaware he was doing anything indiscreet, happened to show Mother the fine ham that Motty had brought him. Father and son were relentlessly interrogated that evening until all was revealed about the dreaded ham. Father could protest truthfully that he'd never laid a finger on the meat but that, according to Mother, was not the point. 'Your unkosher money I do not want!' she bawled and threw two pound notes at my father. 'Better without it than earned in that way! Maurice Zoltie, what kind of a Jew do you call yourself?'

That was the end of Father's dealings with unkosher food. But he was always prepared to bend the rules, ever so slightly, when the profit motive outweighed concern for his soul.

Ham wasn't the only food that got members of the family into trouble. Motty, like me, also experienced problems with fowls. One evening, when he was a teenager, he arrived with about a hundred cockerels in a borrowed van. The birds were to go to market in the morning and it was Motty's intention to let them spend the night in the van, outside our house. One cockerel can rouse a neighbourhood so you can imagine the cacophony that burst upon the quiet street just before dawn as a hundred birds, crowing wildly, vied with one another to announce the arrival of the new day. Windows flew open and furious, dishevelled heads appeared in hairnets and minus dentures. Soon the banging started at the door and Motty was fumbling his way into his

41

trousers. He descended to the street and attempted to soothe the birds but they continued with their chorus. To avoid the wrath of the police, Motty had to climb into the van and drive his whole aviary out of town where he sat in a quiet back road, waiting for the market to open at seven o'clock.

That was not, however, Motty's worst encounter with birds. He was a good story-teller and liked to recount to his friends about the day he ended up in jail, with his chickens:

'Ye see, it was Christmastime and we had two hundred hens in the van when we came back tae the city, when suddenly, "Wham!" A lorry ran intae the back o' us, leavin' a big hole. In nae time at a', there was a terrific flutterin' and cacklin' and the hens were in the street, runnin' in front o' the trams wi' their bells ringin'. Flyin' and squawkin' among children on their way hame frae school, aye, and one or two crafty shoppers whipped a hen or two intae their baskets, and there was *their* Christmas denner. We run aroond, tryin' tae catch them and, suddenly, I saw one flighty wee hen see-sawin' all doon the tramlines and up ontae the bunnet o' a Rolls-Royce. A laughed till the tears run! The Rolls was driven by an upright pan-faced chauffer wi' two elderly gents in the back. The wee hen was cacklin' and pukin' a' over the beautiful shinin' bunnet. A threw maself at it, shoutin' and swearin' and grabbin', while the poor bugger o' a chauffer tried tae look as if nothin' was happenin'. At last a made ma way hame wi' 27 hens missin'. That night a got a message tae go tae the polis station where a foond the polis sergent puce in the face – every five minutes someone had brought in a bloody chicken! "If you're the owner of these bloody hens, go down and collect the lot and get the hell out of here! The smell's awful!" A went doon tae the cells and burst oot laughin'. There were a' the hens, instead o' prisoners, flyin', squawkin' and pukin'. And smellin' awful! They were real jailbirds!'

CHAPTER SEVEN

Fun and Games

Old Joe the Jew, as my father was called, was quite capable of overcoming his religious scruples if there was any chance of indulging in his one great vice – gambling at cards. He couldn't resist poker, pontoon, solo or any game where gelt (money) might be won. Every Sunday, from midday until last thing at night, was time for cards, and every ounce of his calculation and ingenuity went into his fervent efforts to win.

At noon our little house, already overcrowded, became even busier and noisier as Father's friends and gambling cronies shuffled up the stairs and in through the lobby. 'Come on! Come on! What are you all waiting for?' Father would be bitten by the bug and desperate to get started. Everyone had to find a chair quickly as he sat impatiently brandishing his two or three packs of cards. 'Kootky will no be playing, will you Kootky?' This was his standard address to my mother. He went to great pains to protect her from the iniquities of gambling. But she was quite content to take a back seat, if she could find one. Usually, the eager gamblers left her with a box or a bed to sit on.

Anyone who won a game had to deposit the sum of sixpence in Mother's purse. This business-like arrangement meant that the endless supply of tea and sandwiches was adequately paid for. It also ensured that Mother was never allowed to sit for too long!

Those games could never be described as a peaceful way of spending a quiet Sunday afternoon. I still remember the angry cries and indignant shouts.

'You cheated, Maurice Zoltie; you cannot deny it!'
'What! This is a lie!'
'But I saw it. You cheated.'
The noise would build.

'You are a liar. Get oot! Get oot! You must leave my hoose. Nobody calls Maurice Zoltie a liar. Get oot!'

An enraged victim of Father's sometimes devious methods would rise to his feet and stumble unsteadily as the blood returned to his cramped legs. Then he would storm, still protesting, out of the door. But these displays of temper were as much show as anything and a few minutes later the injured party would return, stick his head round the door and say, 'Well, I'll give it one more try. But if you are cheating again – oot I will go and oot I will stay!'

Every time Father was suspected of having had a trick up his sleeve there would be another deafening outburst from one or more of the players. He always protested but sometimes he caught a warning look from my mother and calmed down. It was as if she were saying, without having to open her mouth, 'Oh, be quiet Maurice. You know you are in the wrong.' But sometimes he got completely carried away and would turn bright pink. Insults would fill the room to bursting point, stamping would make the floorboards vibrate and the walls would echo with shouts. Sometimes it would become too much for our long-suffering neighbours.

Then it would come: the ominous knock at the door followed by a sudden petrified silence. 'Oh no! The Polis! Oh, it must be. Somebody's gaffed on us.' Father edged nervously towards the door. He knew his gambling den was illegal and he had to keep the policeman outside the house. He opened the door briskly and stepped out onto the landing, immediately pulling the door shut behind him. We would be able to hear the echoes of his deep voice. Father, being so big, often dwarfed our local policemen.

'Sorry to bother you Mr Zoltie but the neighbours are complaining about the noise again.'

'Noise? Noise?' exclaimed Father self-righteously. 'What do they expect with a family like mine? If I was a farmer, could I stop my sheep bleating?' Then he'd look down kindly at the policeman, 'You must be a family man yourself . . .'. Father always succeeded in calming the storm and the policeman would leave, with Father having promised to try to keep things quieter. But the peace would only last ten minutes, then the players would be hurling accusations at one another again.

I'm sure my father, so strict in so many areas of his life, did cheat at cards, even when he had a game with my mother. Perhaps the enthusiasm he usually displayed in his work was transferred to what ought to have been a harmless pastime and he became obsessed with succeeding, and getting more gelt, no matter how he did it. It was just one more aspect of his survival instinct. His friends must have understood this, because, every Sunday, without fail, they came back for more.

Father wasn't the only person in the family who enjoyed gambling and, though I didn't think much about it at the time, quite a few of my childhood games involved an element of chance. We children rarely had money to spare but we devised our own forms of currency. We had marbles, often referred to as 'bools'. Any modern marbles I've seen tend to look mass-produced and are usually all the same size and design. Our marbles were, in contrast, a varied lot, and so could be regarded as having different values, like coins. There were ones that seemed to be made of stone in colours ranging from a gritty white to liquorice black. There were ones made of solid coloured glass, sometimes chipped, and as big as gobstoppers. And then there were the steelies. I think they were nothing more exotic than ball-bearings but, sparkling and reflecting the sunlight, they were as precious to us as silver.

I don't remember being bought or given any toys. They just happened to be in the house, or we made our own. Sometimes I swapped things with other boys. And, of course, it was always possible to win something. We would place a cardboard shoe-box on the pavement. The box would have four holes cut in it, with the numbers 1, 2, 3 and 4 pencilled above the holes. '1' would be the biggest hole and '4' the smallest. We would roll our

45

marbles along the pavement and try to get them, if possible, into the smallest hole. If successful, then four marbles were won. If your marble rolled into hole '2', you won two marbles. And so on. If, though, you missed all four holes in the box, you lost your own marble. Thus, in the streets, we had our own form of gambling.

Cigarette cards also served as a kind of currency. I would collect them avidly from Father's packets, usually trying to make up complete sets of fifty. There were pictures of famous footballers, cricketers, film stars and racehorses. Usually it was impossible to get a complete set without doing a bit of swapping or bartering. Cigarette cards, like marbles, could be used for games of chance. If someone had a card hidden in his hand, he would say, 'Football team – thirteen letters'. If you managed to guess 'Wolverhampton', you won the card. The cards all had different values as some were much harder to get than others. I'm sure the cigarette companies arranged this deliberately.

A slightly more physical pastime could be indulged in with cigarette cards. One boy would put perhaps twenty cards face down on the pavement. His friend would then blow on them with all his strength and would win all the cards he managed to turn over. Only one breath was allowed and, naturally, this game would leave the participants red-faced and puffing.

We may have been short of pocket money but this didn't curb our imagination. A favourite game was to take the silver paper from cigarette packets, wrap it round a big brown penny and painstakingly rub it until the image of Queen Victoria, King Edward VII or George V began to show through. We then had what looked like half-a-crown (2/6d); we had multiplied our wealth by thirty! Of course, to pass our forgeries in the sweetie shop would have been impossible and we had enough sense not to try.

I associate all these games with the long school holidays which seemed to go on for ever. We couldn't afford to go away but I was happy just to be away from school. It was impossible to be a

boy in Scotland without playing football and, with the King's
Park only minutes away, we didn't have to risk the wrath of the
'polis' by playing in the streets. It seems strange to think of it
now, but we often didn't have a football among us and would
sometimes improvise one with tightly rolled up newspaper and
old bits of string.

The boys and girls rarely played together and I'm sure we
regarded the 'lassies' as inferior beings. A game that, strangely
enough, we did have in common was the making of mud pies in
the back-green. The mud would be easier to work with after
rain, but in the summer, when the ground was hard and dry,
some of the more resourceful boys would urinate on the earth to
produce a more pliable 'dough'.

Another game we shared with the girls was diablo. Some of
them became extremely skilful at rolling and throwing the
specially shaped piece of wood into the air and catching it, using
the string stretched between the two wooden handles. Sometimes the girls played games using marbles. A flat stone would be
thrown into the air and a girl would get to keep as many marbles
as she could pick up before catching the stone on the back of her
hand. The girls also played hopscotch, which we called peevers;
an empty shoe-polish or toothpaste tin would be kicked around a
specially chalked grid on the pavement.

A place I loved to visit, and which was a true fairyland of fun
and games, was my uncle's shop. His name was Myer Schulberg
and he specialised in all kinds of toys and practical jokes. He also
supplied cheap goods to the gipsies and travellers who went
round the doors. I was happy just to sit in his shop with its
exploding cigarettes, stink bombs, false noses and magic tricks. I
think he must have taken his shops on short leases as he always
seemed to be on the move. I can clearly remember visiting him in
The Pleasance and in St Mary's Street, near John Knox's House.

One of the most exciting nights of our year was bonfire night. I
think even the grown-ups quite enjoyed it. Most people associate
bonfires with Guy Fawkes, but our biggest bonfire was in mid

47

May, to celebrate Victoria Day. Two great advantages of this were that the weather was usually reasonable and I could regard the big night as a kind of celebration of my birthday, May 19th. All over Edinburgh the skies were aglow with fires blazing at crossroads and on any patch of waste ground.

There was so little traffic at that time that the police allowed us to spend days building up our mountain of junk in the roadway. We used to go round the doors collecting anything that would burn. We must have burnt many an old piece of furniture which today would have fetched a good price in the trendy second-hand furniture shops.

On the night, the grey street would be transformed into a wonderland of sparks and shadows. Excited faces would reflect the red glow as catherine-wheels whirred and rockets whooshed into the dark sky. Dogs yelped as bangers exploded and wood cracked loudly in the fire. Sometimes, if it was windy, sparks would be blown unexpectedly into an open window and the curtains would begin to smoulder. Then the climax of the night would be the noisy arrival of a fire-engine.

As the night wore on and the bonfire sagged into a flattened heap of embers, some of us would risk a scorching to bury potatoes in the ash. They were rarely properly cooked but that mixture of earth, charcoal and hard potato tasted magnificent. Eventually we would be called home with our hands and mouths blackened and our hair and clothes reeking like a kippery.

Bonfire night was one of the few celebrations shared by the Scots and the Jewish families. There was a day trip that we, like many of our Scottish neighbours, enjoyed immensely: going to Portobello on the tram. In those days, a two or three mile journey down to the seaside seemed like an expedition. We'd walk to Waterloo Place and board the tram from the island in the middle of the road.

When I was young the Edinburgh trams were pulled by a cable beneath the road – a method entirely free from pollution! In the early 1920s the electric trams took over, drawing their power from a network of overhead cables which sometimes sparked dramatically. We children loved best to travel upstairs in the open air, on the hard wooden seats.

The driver had a bell which he could ring with his foot and there was a constant clanging as he warned pedestrians of his approach. Sitting on top of the tram, in all weathers, was almost like sailing through the city in a high ship. We loved it. When we reached the terminus the driver used to remove his big driving-wheel from its stanchion and carry it to the other end of the tram for the return journey.

Enterprising schoolboys would search the floors of the trams for tickets which had not been punched. They could be carefully smoothed out to look like new and could be sold for a penny a dozen.

At the end of our tram trip was Portobello, then a thriving holiday resort with an impressive golden beach. Most of us would take along our own tea and sandwiches – only the well-to-do could afford the luxury of going to cafés. The beach would be packed and we'd paddle in the icy waters of the Firth of Forth. To all of us, a fortnight in Spain would have seemed an impossible dream.

Big dances used to take place every week at the Marine Gardens in Portobello and people came from all over the city. As a boy I was drawn towards the fun-fair on the promenade and longed for a 'go' on the scenic railway. When I was a bit older, and the family had a car, Mother set up a little stall with a folding table on the prom and made some extra cash by selling dolls, toys, jumping-beans and bric-a-brac, while we swam or played.

Back at St Leonard's Hill, on the long, light summer evenings, street singers used to come round and sometimes went into the back-greens to sing. They were really begging and the house-wives, knowing how hard up they must be, would throw pennies from the windows. I've heard that less charitable folk would sometimes heat the pennies until they were almost red hot and enjoy a cruel laugh as the singers burnt their fingers trying to

49

pick up the coins. I particularly remember one would-be enter-tainer. He only seemed to know one line which sounded to me like, 'Dougal Donald, he's my friend; Dougal Donald, he's my friend,' over and over again. He played the spoons as he sang his endless song. I think people gave him money out of pity.

The fun and games filled our Easter and summer holidays but always, inevitably, the time came for the dreaded return to St Leonard's Primary. I knew the time was near when I saw new blazers on the dummies in the window of the Co-op. Then the awful morning would arrive and I'd set off up St Leonard's Hill, with my boots newly polished, to battle with sums and spelling. Again I'd feel like the odd one out as I sat among all the children my parents referred to as the Christians. I'd stare longingly out of the high windows and pray I was somewhere else as I breathed in the dull smells of ink and chalk-dust. We sat on long forms behind sparse desks of old, dark wood. Big metal radiators stood round the walls, like sentries, guarding over us.

That school is now gone. Long grass and wild flowers flourish in its empty space.

CHAPTER EIGHT

More Memories of Motty

Fear of Father's temper tended to keep us in some kind of order. We were all aware of the existence of his leather belt. And we all used this fear in order to exercise a form of blackmail over one another. I'll give an example.

Motty and Karl were planning a picnic and Lena wanted to go with them. But they didn't want a mere girl and refused to allow her to go along. She was bitterly disappointed but didn't know what to do about it. Until, a little later, she found them pretending to be strongmen. They'd recently been to a local theatre and seen a man doing an act with dumb-bells. They were so impressed by this that they'd found some lemonade bottles to use as substitute weights and were grimacing, posing and posturing their way through their version of the strongman's act, in the kitchen. Lena, unaware of these domestic theatricals, burst through the door and was promptly rendered unconscious by one of the improvised dumb-bells. Motty and Karl were overcome with panic, fearing that they'd put an end to their sister's earthly existence. They patted her cheeks and rubbed her hands in a desperate effort to restore her to life. Then, suddenly, she sat up, quite unaffected by the blow. But now, of course, she had a trump card to play. Either she went along on the picnic or Father would be told about her being nearly killed and the big leather belt would swing into action. Lena went on the picnic.

I've suggested that Motty was the most streetwise of the family. He was never short of schemes for getting gelt and he was sometimes less than particular about how he managed it. At Hallowe'en, Scottish children go guising – they dress up and sing songs for money. It's a very old custom but should only be done on 31st October. Motty saw nothing wrong with trying this at other times of the year and once, when the American fleet was at Leith Docks, he took Lena guising. He was making quite a bit of money from the bemused sailors, until a passing policeman decided that my brother and sister were begging. Father, furious, had to collect them from the police station. In fact, Father was so hard on them that the police thought it unnecessary to press charges.

With Motty, it was not solely the desire for money which motivated his escapades. He seemed to enjoy taking a risk. But he didn't always realise that he might be causing distress to others. We sometimes got our bread and rolls from a Russian emigré baker called Mr Plansey. While Motty was still attending school he used to do some delivering for the baker.

Mr Plansey was a pale, fat man with a fat wife and six fat children. By modern standards, his premises were incredibly cramped and probably unhygienic. Moreover the Planseys seemed destitute. They had a front shop with a kitchen behind. Between the two areas were two big cupboards – they weren't grand enough to be described as boxrooms. These had no light, and it was in them that the eight Planseys somehow slept, in four beds.

In spite of his living conditions, Mr Plansey produced wonderful bread and rolls which Motty delivered to the Jewish customers. But the straightforward delivery of the bags was not enough to keep Motty amused; he used to remove a roll from some of the bags, thus leaving the customers short. It never occurred to him that Mr Plansey was bound to get complaints. Motty used to bring all his 'extra' rolls home to Mother with a story about them being left over at the end of the day.

At first Mr Plansey took the blame for making the bags up wrongly, but eventually Motty's villainy was uncovered and he got the sack. He apparently saw no disgrace in this but had, of course, to contend with the wrath of Father.

Motty must have been a continual source of irritation to Father but my brother never seemed to care about what other people thought of him. Once, when he couldn't find his rubber shoes, he played a game of football, and scored a goal, in a pair of ladies' shoes with raised heels. The rest of us would have settled for playing in our bare feet. But not Motty.

Motty's choice of friends even caused us trouble. There was one called Henry who sometimes stayed the night with us. This made our bed particularly crowded and matters did not improve when one morning we couldn't stop scratching. This was not an unusual state of affairs as we used to get fleas from the chickens. We'd also get nits in our hair and Father used to give us regular top-to-toe examinations in search of unwanted guests. He was an expert at cracking these little marauders between his finger-nails.

But after Henry's visit, Father could find none of the regular culprits on our bodies and still we itched and clawed at ourselves. Reluctantly, he decided to seek professional advice, which meant spending some hard-earned gelt. In our area, people only called the doctor as a last resort. Fortunately, our family kept reasonably healthy and any minor complaint would be treated with bowls of pease brose – a very dark porridge made with oatmeal and peas.

The tiny white pimples between our fingers were not, however, going to react to pease brose. Henry had given us all scabies. We were marched to the Royal Infirmary, stripped and larded with sulphur ointment. We had to put our clothes on again on top of the smelly, sticky goo and it was wretchedly uncomfortable. The itch was eventually banished – as was Motty's friend who was never allowed to darken our front door again.

CHAPTER NINE

More Tales of Vices

Any sudden extra expenditure would seriously disrupt our meagre housekeeping budget. That was why a visit to the doctor would be avoided if possible. It was worse in the winter when Father found it more difficult to do his rounds in the often grim Scottish weather. Also, he was prone to bronchitis and sometimes was just too unwell to face the elements, loaded down with his packs. The fact that he was a heavy smoker didn't help. Sometimes he would start to speak but his sentence would sink without trace in an outburst of wheezing and coughing. But he stubbornly refused to abandon his cigarettes. Mother attacked him from two fronts, pointing out the cost in money and the toll on his health. 'How much profit goes up in flames?' she would ask him. 'The children need food and you smoke!'

'Kootky, Kootky,' he would protest. 'What have I got? This is my only pleasure. I *like* cigarettes. Leave me alone.'

His poor health was of course hastening the day when it would be necessary for his eldest sons to have to go out on the road, even if it meant interrupting their education.

Cigarettes were not, as we've seen, my father's only pleasure. He loved gambling and followed the horses. Mother didn't object to this piece of indulgence and was even known to risk sixpence each way, out of the housekeeping. Father's bets were modest, too, but he loved to scrutinise the form in a newspaper. Mother was a staunch believer in a tipster known as Captain Colt. It was my job to take the wagers and the betting-slips to the bookie who, at that time, operated illegally. He was usually to be found lurking shiftily in a dark stair or shadowy corner. At the end of the day he would be made conspicuous by a small crowd of men looking for their winnings but there was usually a look-out posted nearby to watch for the 'rozzers' – the men in blue.

With my inherited instinct for making money, it wasn't long before I started to take an interest in the little scraps of paper I was carrying back and forward. I concluded that my parents weren't making a very good job of it; I could do better. I started to select my own nag from the daily paper but, as usual, I had no money. I was convinced, like all gamblers, that I would win, so I confidently helped myself to some of Father's money, for my stake. That wasn't easy as he not only had his bag of sixpences, shillings and half-crowns in a locked drawer, he also hid the key to the drawer. After much searching, my fingers tingled with excitement when I located his key on a high shelf.

At first, I helped myself to a few shillings, then carefully selected my horses. I had as much luck as my parents. Never mind, I thought. I'm bound to win next time. I was hooked. Back to the locked drawer I went and dipped into the bag for more coins. And again and again.

Father must have become suspicious about my painstaking study of the racing pages. Anyway, I'm sure he began to keep an eye on me because, one morning, just as I slid my fingers into his money-bag, I felt the unmistakable grip of his strong hand clamp down on my shoulder. The game was over. Down came the dreaded leather belt again and little Hymie was soon learning yet another lesson about life. The key went into a new hiding place.

I wasn't the only member of the family to fall foul of the horses. One of my older brothers actually became a bookie at the racecourse. His career began and ended on the same afternoon. He was convinced, as are most punters, that the bookie never lost, so he set up his own stand. Unfortunately, he wasn't content just to do as well as the other bookies; he wanted to do much better. So he offered more attractive odds, based on his hope that the favourite horse in each race wouldn't win. People flocked round him, putting as much as they could afford on the favourites. And in every race, with sickening regularity, the favourite came in first. As the afternoon wore on, my brother got paler and paler. Eventually an angry crowd gathered round him, demanding their winnings. Of course my brother couldn't pay them. He'd taken a gamble, and lost. He had a hasty conference with my father which ended in IOUs being handed out and my brother returning home in debt, his entrepreneurial spirit considerably dampened.

It was as a result of my father's ingenuity that my brother had been at the race course in the first place. Father knew that a lot of bookies had to get from the city centre to the track so he hired a bus, charged them fares, and took them all together. This meant, naturally, that *he* got to the meeting free, and, if all went according to plan, he made a little profit on the deal. Unfortunately, if the bookies had a bad day, he had to make do with only vague promises: 'Oh, we'll pay ye double next time,' they would insist. So even Father's Bookies' Bus became something of a gamble for him. I don't think he would have enjoyed it any other way!

CHAPTER TEN

Trial and Error

Edinburgh's Calton Hill is noted for its monuments to Lord Nelson and Robert Burns. It also boasts an observatory, the original Royal High School building and the grave of David Hume. Moreover, through most of the nineteenth and early twentieth century, it was the site of the Calton Jail. Jessie King became infamous as the last woman to be hanged there, in 1889. And to the dismay of us all, Father was one day carted off to the Calton Jail. It wasn't because he was a wanton criminal; it was just that he hadn't realised he was doing anything illegal. So he ended up keeping company with thieves and murderers. I'd better explain how this came about.

On his many trips around the countryside, Father inevitably became friendly with a number of café proprietors, particularly in Fife. He persuaded some of them that it would be in their interests to instal penny-in-the-slot fruit machines for gambling and he helped them to arrange the rentals. This was all very well until Father devised a small gambling scheme using the machines. It was a harmless entertainment involving some of the café regulars and nobody thought very much about it. Father in his innocence had no idea he was contravening the gaming laws but the local police found out, seized all the fruit machines and put him in court where he was found guilty and fined heavily. We had no ready money so, to his horror, Father found himself locked away in the Calton Jail.

I was too young to visit him but heard he was sharing a cell with a murderer who had thrown his victim out of a tenement window. The diet consisted mostly of black bread and water.

My mother tried to raise money from the neighbours to speed his release but most were far too poor to help. The rabbi helped a little but, in the end, what she collected only reduced Father's sentence by a few days.

Once out and about again, Father continued on his enterprising way with his accustomed energy. But he kept well away from gambling machines. On his long-distance expeditions he penetrated to areas where there were no trains or buses. This meant there was little competition for him. If he was carrying a lot of stock, he might make use of a taxi and would do his best to pay the fare with balloons, watches, rings or contraceptives. If he couldn't find a farmer, he directed his sales talk at the farmer's wife, tempting her with a display of clothes and jewellery.

Being used to poverty himself, Father would be lenient with some of his customers who were often hard up. I think he was one of the first people to deal regularly on a credit basis and would collect a few pence at a time from some of his customers. This inevitably made things more difficult for us but his credit system worked reasonably until the General Strike of 1926. Then it collapsed. He was owed money by hundreds of people who didn't have a farthing to pay him. Father looked around in desperation for a new means of feeding his hungry family.

Harry Glass was in the wholesale fruit and vegetable trade at the time and Father was friendly with him. Both were members of the same masonic lodge. Harry heard of Father's difficulties and tried to help. He knew there was a shop vacant with a cheap rent. It was in the Grassmarket, in Edinburgh's Old Town. Parts of this area have since been gentrified but at that time it was very poor indeed and a place some people would avoid walking in after dark. Still, business was business wherever it was, so Father made up his mind to have a go at being a grocer. Harry Glass supplied fruit and vegetables on a long-term credit basis and enough cash was scraped together to line the shelves with such basic items as sugar, salt, tea, tinned goods and cigarettes. We were all optimistic about our latest venture.

I can remember the shop as being unbelievably tiny (which accounted for the small rent) but, as the area was busy, Father had what seemed like a good position and reasonable prospects of success. For years the Grassmarket has been known for its lodging-houses, used by men, young and old, who have fallen on hard times; there also used to be quite a number of Irishmen over here for casual labour. Some people would have had their doubts about such a prospective clientele but we soon found that poverty has its own economics.

As the men had very little money, they would buy one or two slices of bread at a time, for a penny or twopence. Sugar and tea was sold in one-ounce bags and cigarettes were sold as 'singles' rather than in packets. Though this involved much pernickety weighing and wrapping, Father found himself doing quite well. (I believe that even if the customers had enough money for larger amounts, they couldn't risk it as theft was a continual risk in the lodging-houses.)

Father, as always, was on the alert for new ideas with which to increase his profits. One day I wandered into the shop sucking a toffee apple. I laid my sticky treat down on Father's counter and he started to shout at me about the mess. Then, suddenly, he stopped and began to study the offending item. He seemed puzzled but interested as he sniffed and poked at it. 'Goot Got! Well, well. . . .'

That evening he announced to Mother that we were going into the toffee apple business and we would be making them ourselves! He had a case of apples which were drying up and crinkly, so he would use these.

Next day an old fruit crate was cut into thin sticks. The remainder of the wood was used to help build a big fire. Father and Mother crouched over a pot, stirring an aromatic mixture of hot water and brown sugar. I felt quietly proud. I knew that *my* toffee apple was the inspiration behind this latest venture. All that had to be done was pierce the apples with the sticks, dip them in the mixture, then leave them to harden. The toffee apples were a success and became one of Father's most popular lines. The only problem was that, as they lay on the counter on display, their naked sweetness attracted flies, whose legs would adhere to the sticky coating. Father hung up long strips of flypaper but Ella and I discovered what, we thought, was a better solution. We squatted beside the counter and, when Father was busy elsewhere, we nicked the trespassing flies off with our penknives.

I used to go to the shop after school to see if Father needed any help. If there was nothing to be done, I used to sit under the counter, so as not to clutter up the tiny shop; my space was quite a comfortable little cubby-hole. I used to hide and listen to the customers and the sound of the till drawer. Before long, I discovered that it was possible from where I sat to manoeuvre my hand through a two-inch gap and into the back of the drawer, without anyone seeing. I regularly helped myself to a little money. I always spent this before I got home as I knew what would happen if money were discovered in my pockets. I have to admit that that particular crime continued to pay. Father was the worst of accountants and never noticed any shortages in his days' takings.

In spite of my malpractices, the shop did fairly well but before long the fresh spring air began to drift in through the narrow doorway and Father's feet got restless. His wanderlust was returning. He found the shop claustrophobic and began to tire of it. He missed his long journeys to the countryside and the excitement of bargaining. His solution was to employ a Scots girl, or a sheeksy, as we Jews would say. This allowed him to get away and see his farmers, but not for long.

One of the family used to go to the Grassmarket every evening to collect the takings. After a while, Father discovered he had a pile of unpaid bills from wholesalers and hardly any money from the shop, though it had been busy. He suspected the sheeksy. A trap was set with marked bank notes and she was caught and duly sacked.

But a lot of money had been taken and Father felt compelled to return to the shop to straighten out the business. But his heart wasn't in it. He was longing for the open road.

Though always on the look-out for increased profits, Father could at times display a generosity at odds with his business sense. An old man would come in for a slice of bread and Father would put two in the bag. He would give bananas or sweeties to the children. He never forgot his own poverty.

Then something happened which finally finished Father with the shop. It became known in the family as that 'cigarette business'. At the time, Capstan, Father's favourite brand, were selling for a shilling a packet. One day, a stranger came in and offered Capstan cigarettes to Father at sixpence a packet. Father bought the lot, several cartons, then rushed home to tell Mother about his deal. He sold them cheaply in order to undercut the other shops. Business was good.

But before long, two detectives were peering through the doorway and eventually their presence filled the tiny shop. They eyed the packets of Capstan and they eyed Father. 'I'm sorry,' one of them said. 'We'll have to take the cigarettes away.'

'What do you mean? I pay a good price for them,' Father protested indignantly. But it was no use. He was soon on his way to the police station again. Once more, he was in trouble with the law.

The charge officer knew Father. Both men were members of the Solomon Lodge of masons. 'What have you been doing now, Old Joe?' the officer inquired.

'Look,' replied Father. 'I buy, I sell. That is my life. That's all I do. What is wrong?'

The cigarettes were stolen goods and the police confiscated the lot. Father was out-of-pocket but gave the police what information he could and avoided a return trip to jail. Even so, he felt he hadn't done anything wrong. He hadn't stolen the cigarettes, after all. The worry of this episode disillusioned him and hurried the end of his brief career as a shopkeeper. He put up the shutters and let his thoughts turn towards the open country.

CHAPTER ELEVEN

On The Road

In the summer months it was Father's habit to visit the various agricultural shows held throughout rural Scotland. For a small trading fee, people like Father were allowed to sell almost anything – watches, rings, jewellery, even balloons.

Between the age of twelve and fourteen, I became quite familiar with these shows. Of course, I should have been attending school but Father was the boss and business came first. It was better, he reckoned, that his sons should be out earning gelt than that he should be wasting gelt buying books for school.

We all had to write our own letters to the school, explaining our habitual absences. It was a good training in forgery. I can still remember writing, 'Please excuse Hymie from lessons today. . .'. Naturally, the attendance officer noticed our absences. We were a healthy-looking bunch so it made our repeated claims to illness all the more suspect. The attendance officer decided to visit the Zoltie household to offer his commiserations. The place was deserted. We were all away at an agricultural show.

Father was warned that his children must attend school but in spite of the watchful eye of the authorities I clocked up a fair number of working days before I was legally able to leave school.

Father was in his element at the shows, always devising new ways of selling. He'd hook up one of his stock of watches to his own chain to make the public believe he was prepared to sell his very own watch to them. He put extra rings on to make people believe they were buying his own valuable property, from his own fingers.

I was too young to deal with important items like watches and rings. I was delegated to the balloons. Unfortunately, the wretched things had to be blown up first and I used to exhaust myself blowing my way through the multi-coloured heap of limp rubber. Then I realised that the bellows from our fireplace did a more effective job, so these would go on tour with us throughout the summer.

At first I stood around, waiting for customers. Business was slow. Father soon put me right. I had to use initiative. The best method was to look out for a mother and child, get close to them, then make sure a bright balloon on a stick was within the child's sticky grasp. The child would make a grab for it and once it had the stick it yelled blue murder if anyone tried to take the balloon away. The mother had no choice but to pay up.

I soon got wise to this way of selling but there was one aspect of my early career in balloons which used to puzzle me. Sometimes a big farmer would sidle up and ask how much the balloons were. Dutifully I would answer, 'The big ones are fourpence and the wee ones are threepence.'

'Och, dinnae be sae daft!' the disgruntled farmer would reply, then move away in search of Father.

One day another farmer approached me, nervously. 'Could I hae a gross, son?' he asked. I must have looked amazed. 'One hundred and forty four,' he explained. 'You know what a gross is, laddie?' I nodded and started to count out the variously coloured balloons. The farmer became annoyed. 'Och, you know whit I'm talkin' aboot. It's the rubber goods I'm lookin' for – a gross!' Then he too went looking for Father.

What I didn't know, in all my innocence, was that Father was doing a healthy trade in contraceptives. In his casual conversations with taxi drivers, railway porters and farmers, he'd often heard them joke about the troubles they had looking after their big families. He discovered that many of these men were just too embarrassed to go to the chemist and buy contraceptives over the counter. So their families grew and grew in size. Father solved their problems by supplying the desired 'rubber goods' discreetly at the agricultural shows. But he hadn't bothered to tell me!

While I was being initiated into the mysteries of family planning, my older brothers, Motty, Karl and Reuben, were busy taking photographs. They watched out for the prize-winning horses, sheep, bulls and cows, then photographed the beasts with their owners. The owners were usually so proud that they happily bought several copies of each picture. 'Two shillings each or a set of six for ten shillings,' was the cry. This was always good business but, when my brothers photographed the winning entries in the Women's Institute cake-making competition, the pictures didn't sell at all. The women seemed much less susceptible to the Zoltie patter.

Our travels took us as far as the islands. On one occasion, my brothers heard about an agricultural show on a small island which could be reached by boat from Oban. They didn't know what to expect but, ever hopeful, they made the trip, hoping for good business. After paying their fares then scouring the island, they found one tiny pen containing a horse, a cow and two sheep.

Eventually, about a hundred people gathered from all over the island for the big event and, naturally, they all saw the horse and the cow each winning a first prize. There were ferocious arguments among the judges about the two sheep but eventually everything was settled amicably and my brothers did excellent business photographing various islanders with various beasts. The Women's Temperance Association had a display of food and vegetables and Karl, who loved turnips, had an extremely good feed. Then in the middle of the jollifications Motty looked up and shouted, 'There's the bloody boat – it's away!' And sure enough, their boat was steaming steadily on its return journey to the mainland. The brothers were marooned.

There was, however, a solution. A phone call to the mainland would bring a tiny boat out across the water. The postmaster stood by, smiling; he was a tall, striking figure with long red hair. He spoke only Gaelic and seemed unable to understand my brothers' distress.

As they waited for the boat, the skies darkened and the seas rose. At first, my brothers were worried about having to spend their takings on the special boat hire. In the end, they were grateful to reach dry land after a hair-raising trip through mountainous waves. After that, they were considerably less interested in venturing to the islands in search of business.

Father believed that every day could be a good day for business. His sons were sometimes less convinced. Morning prayers would involve asking God to bless the day and bring good rewards but sometimes, it seemed, God wasn't listening. Motty told us of such a day when he almost gave up hope. He was at a show but nobody seemed interested in being photographed. As usual, Motty sought out the owners of the prize-winning beasts but couldn't get any orders. Feeling depressed, he began to pack his equipment. Then, out of the corner of his eye, he saw a tiny fellow march by with a huge sheepdog. And the dog was sporting a first-prize ticket on its collar.

'Excuse me,' said Motty, pointing at his camera, without much hope.

'Aye! Sure!' replied the shepherd.

The click of the shutter seemed to hypnotise him. Motty photographed him with the dog sitting and with the dog lying down. Then the shepherd sat while the dog stood. Then the dog begged. The shepherd whistled and the shepherd pointed while the dog went through its repertoire of tricks. Then, incredibly, all the shepherd's family and friends arrived and the whole business started over again. By the time he got away, Motty had done one of his best day's business. God had perhaps been listening after all.

The camera my father and brothers used was an Aptus. I believe Father was the first photographer to use it in Scotland. It was considered revolutionary at the time, as photographs could be taken then developed while the customer waited. The novelty value of this helped to ensure regular business. The camera was a big box of a thing, mounted on a tripod. It contained fifty small tin plates, each wrapped in paper. The camera also contained its own soaking device. At first, however, there was a major problem. If the finished photograph was left in strong light, it began to fade within a day or two. I'm pleased to say that Father later devised a means of making the prints permanent.

CHAPTER TWELVE

Wheeling and Dealing

I've mentioned that Father could be generous. When money was flowing in, he loved to give Kootky sweets or flowers. Sometimes we got a treat to compensate for an earlier burst of temper. But when it came to the family being partners in business, there was no generosity at all. Every farthing had to be accounted for. After the agricultural shows, all the takings had to be dutifully handed over to Father. Then he would give my brothers their allowance of spending money. But not until he'd searched their pockets to confirm their honesty. Also, from time to time, he'd search any known hiding places in the house. His suspicions were not groundless. My brothers, particularly Motty, racked their brains for new ways to hoodwink him. For a while Motty managed to conceal some money in his socks. But Father found it, even there, and exploded. 'Why the hell you hide the money in the socks? They are filthy, stinking socks!' However, Motty did eventually find the perfect place: he used to unscrew the brass knobs from the corners of our bed and insert pound notes, rolled up like cigarettes. He'd finally outwitted Father.

But Father never gave up his battle with Motty. Before they went to a show, Father issued Motty with a precise number of photographic plates. Back home in the evening, Father would check inside the camera to see how many were unused. In order not to expose the plates, he had to carry out his detective work in our unlit lavatory. He would then know how much money Motty should have earned. But Motty, being his own flesh and blood, was just as cunning: he simply bought a supply of plates from a wholesaler and stuck them in the camera before coming home. So Father could never ascertain just how much money Motty had made.

Travelling round the country as we did, it was necessary to stay overnight in boarding-houses. Our choice was influenced partly by price and partly by the fact that we took our own food with us. I can remember staying in one at Turriff, near Aberdeen, with Karl, Motty, Reuben and Father. It was run by a Church of Scotland minister and his wife.

One evening, Father and my brothers were playing solo whist after their long day's work. In burst the minister to complain about the amount of noise. When he saw the cards he turned purple and accused us of having desecrated his house. Having witnessed many a card game at home, I viewed these proceedings with interest. The minister stormed out and returned with the local policeman. The officer stood surveying the scene, a family game of cards. He rubbed his chin for a few moments then turned to the enraged minister to announce, 'A canna dae much aboot the cairds as long as they keep quiet.'

This judgement wasn't good enough for the minister, though he waited until the following morning to pronounce sentence on us. The atmosphere was tense. When Father asked for the bill, he got what was, for him, a pleasant surprise. 'Get out of my house and never come back,' snarled the minister. 'I will not accept money from heathens!'

It was not only our 'heathen' ways which upset the owners of boarding-houses. Once, we arrived back in Edinburgh to find several angry letters, including one from a solicitor. The solicitor was demanding that Father pay for the replacement of some bed linen. One of the other letters referred delicately to someone 'passing water in the night'. I'm afraid that I was the 'someone'. I suffered from a weak bladder and was therefore not the best of guests to have in a boarding-house. Father paid up and, ever-practical, invested in a rubber sheet for us to carry around Scotland. In the end, he had to accept that my weak bladder was a liability and he became less willing to take me on trips.

But meanwhile, the twentieth century was marching on and our old methods of travelling were becoming more impractical.

The trains were often slow and there were long waits for connections. Our stock of goods grew and became increasingly cumbersome. There was also all the heavy paraphernalia of the photography business to lug around. Father considered buying a car; it was more a necessity than a luxury.

Our first family car was a Morris Cowley. Father got it from one of his farmer friends. It was decrepit, with a canvas roof that leaked. The tyres were threadbare and the windows made of canvas and a yellowed plastic material which, presumably, had been transparent when the car was new. The doors were secured with string. It had cost Father a gold signet ring and a watch. It became known to the neighbours as the Zoltic Sports Special, perhaps because only a good sport would risk riding in it.

The car proved a dubious bargain. On our first excursion it broke down an hour outside Edinburgh. Motty had been telling us how well he understood engines. But, when it came to the crunch, he lifted the bonnet and didn't know where to begin. So, sweating and swearing, the rest of us helped him push the car back to Edinburgh while Father steered.

Breakdowns were quite common and they could affect our business badly. Sometimes we would be two or three hours late for a show and that would make a big dent in our takings. If we arrived too late to see the prizes being awarded for the livestock, we missed the best chances for photography business. Father's solution to this new problem was starting out earlier. So, grumbling and protesting, we could be seen rattling away from St Leonard's Hill at four in the morning.

I remember these early morning excursions as being cold and miserable, even in July and August. The car was well ventilated: chilly winds came through every crack and the old canvas roof was no protection. Our teeth chattered and our feet grew stiff. Then the sky would darken and rain would patter noisily on the roof. It was only a matter of minutes before it was landing on us. Father decided that some money would have to be spent on improvements. So he went out and bought an umbrella. Whenever it rained, we sat in our car, huddled under the umbrella, slowly grinding our way along the lonely Highland roads. Whenever Motty drove, the drips seemed to run off the umbrella and down the back of his neck. This led to the inevitable shouting match – something else which makes me look back on my early days of motoring with less than relish.

On one journey, from Mallaig to Inverness, the road was particularly grim. Time after time, Motty produced his 'wee outfit' for doing repairs to the tyres and tubes. In the end, there were more patches than anything else and it looked as though we were going to be stranded. But our entrepreneurial spirit saved the day: we stuffed the tyres with grass. It did for a while but when we finally rolled down the main street of Inverness, sparks were flying from the rims of the wheels.

After the summer season was over, the car had taken such a battering on the narrow roads and cobbled streets that Father thought we should put it in store for the winter. He said flatly that he couldn't afford the bills for more repairs. Motty, however, with a gleam in his eye, said that he saw no reason why the car shouldn't be used for pleasure as well as business. 'Why not use it,' he suggested to Karl, 'for dating the broads?'

So one night, at the local dance hall, Motty and Karl arranged to take two unsuspecting girls on a day trip to the coast the following Sunday. Motty spent all his free time patching and repairing our Sports Special but when the girls set eyes on it they appeared horrified. I suppose they'd expected a normal car.

The girls were splendidly turned out in the short skirts which were fashionable at the time. One wore a Mexican-style hat and white fur. Both sported another fashion of the time – garters with little bells which tinkled as they walked.

They had to be persuaded to get into the Morris. Anxiously, Motty started the engine and they were on their way. The morning was mercifully dry but cold. Soon the draughts were sweeping in through every crack. The girls shivered. The brothers' forced jollity didn't help.

70

Eventually, they reached North Berwick, where the east wind was cutting its way in from the North Sea. The girls spotted a rather grand-looking Victorian hotel and quickly decided they needed a couple of brandies. This sent Karl and Motty scuttling to the Gents for a hurried consultation. 'I don't fancy them much – their tastes are too bloody expensive,' they concluded.

The girls had their brandy, then were startled to find they were being hustled back into the car. Just when they'd begun to get comfortable! The dark clouds were forming and the brothers became doubly anxious (neither had thought to bring along the umbrella). Before long the rain was streaming and the old wheels were churning up the water and mud. The journey back was a nightmare. The girls were furious as they sat there helpless as the water poured in on their best clothes.

After that outing, Karl and Motty decided that broads should be taken to the local cinema and the Sports Special should be reserved for business trips only.

In the early years of visiting the agricultural shows, we nearly always did well, in spite of the car. But after a time, word got about that there were business possibilities at the shows and we began to face some strange competition. Some of the newcomers described themselves as 'speciality salesmen'. Often they were selling junk at inflated prices. Some held auctions. I can remember people going around begging. There were women with shawl-covered babies. Pickpockets began to appear and there were odd acts such as Reggie the Razor Strop King and his Talking Dog. All this made our life more difficult.

One of the biggest problems was caused by the groups of slick-talking photographers who began to come up from England. With their quick patter, they soon got the farmers to part with their money. These photographers promised to send expensive colour enlargements through the post but, needless to say, the photographs rarely materialised. The farmers were fleeced.

As the undesirable element among the traders increased,

there were complaints from the farmers and soon all tradesmen were banned, including us.

Father wasn't one to give up easily so we still went to Highland games and fairs. We replaced our air-filled balloons with gas ones which floated through the air. But even these caused trouble as we had to carry a large cylinder around with us and some people found it fun to throw cigarette ends at the balloons and make them explode.

My brothers continued with the photography but there were no prize-winning animals at the games and fairs, so there was less business all round. My brothers took pictures of people having picnics or standing beside their cars but there just wasn't the same demand.

Some hard thinking had to be done. In the end, Father admitted there was little point in continuing to go out on the road. So he joined forces with Reuben and opened up a little shop in a side street in Edinburgh. But they weren't going to sell tea and sugar, or even watches and rings. Father knew from experience that there was one product which was always in demand and decided that the Zolties should satisfy that demand. So Reuben found himself behind the counter in a medical supplies shop, selling contraceptives to the male population of Edinburgh.

The shop was discreetly situated; trade flourished.

CHAPTER THIRTEEN

Love and Leaving

Though my older brothers were kept occupied with Father's various ventures, it was inevitable that they found time for girls. Matchmaking was still common in the Jewish community. It was important to make a 'good' match and a professional matchmaker could earn a fair commission from arranging a 'suitable' marriage. When Motty was nineteen, Mother tried to arrange a marriage for him. He was taken to Glasgow to meet the girl and her respectable family. But Motty, true to character, would have none of it. He came back to Edinburgh complaining that the girl was a 'tall skinny lump'. Then he added, to make his position quite clear, 'A'll go single all my days before A'll marry *her*!'

Nor would Reuben have anything to do with matchmaking. He went totally against the tradition by falling in love with an extremely non-Jewish, Spanish senorita. Father could hardly object to her being foreign but the shocking fact that she was a Catholic could have been too much for him to bear. And Reuben was a member of the synagogue choir!

Reuben dated her in secret but, as they wanted to get married, the terrible truth would have to come out. In the end, things were settled reasonably amicably. The girl wasn't strongly attached to her Catholicism and agreed to accept the Jewish faith. This meant she went to the Sabbath service on Friday evenings and got instruction from the rabbi.

After the service, Reuben would bring her home with him. It was one of the few occasions when our house was reduced to silence. We were struck dumb by there actually being a sheeksy among us. I think Father must have found these subdued evenings a little hard to take because, one night, he went to rather strange lengths to liven things up.

We were all used to strong smells around the house but that evening we all began to glance at one another accusingly. There was an unusually powerful odour in the room. Our visitor appeared not to notice. She was either very polite or had a very defective sense of smell. Eventually, Reuben, perhaps embarrassed by the growing stench, burst out, 'Who the hell is stinking?' He looked at Father. We all thought Father would be furious but, surprisingly, he fell about laughing and pointed across the kitchen to the recess where his bed was. We thought he was making a reference to the chamber-pot which was kept underneath the bed, but Karl shouted out, 'It's no' that!' We all knew what a chamber-pot smelled like; the smell in the room was something we *didn't* recognise. Still laughing, Father got a long-handled brush and poked under the bed with it. To our horror, something brown and spiky came scurrying out. Mother and the girls were terrified and jumped onto chairs, screaming hysterically. Someone shouted, 'Don't touch it!' Another voice yelled, 'It's poisonous!' But Father just laughed.

'Why vorry, why vorry? It's only a hedgehog,' he explained. But his strange practical joke backfired. Mother wouldn't speak to him for two days. And Reuben's senorita must have wondered about what kind of family she was marrying into. Father's response was to ask, 'Why is it just my sons who have all the fun? Why can't I enjoy myself too?'

Reuben, for one, certainly knew how to enjoy himself. He was always enthusiastic about any new craze, be it a dance or style of clothing. I can remember how someone donated an out-of-tune piano to our already ridiculously noisy household and Reuben used to practise his dancing while one of us beat out a discordant approximation of some popular tune. When the fashion for Oxford bags was just beginning, Reuben came into the house wearing new trousers which almost hid his feet. The effect was completed by a straw boater. Reuben must have thought he was the bee's knees but Father nearly threw him out of the house.

'You look like a bloody woman!' he shouted. The message was getting to Father that just because his kids were growing up, they weren't becoming any less troublesome to him.

As our dark-skinned sister Betty grew, so did her liking for coloured boys. And when she arrived home with one, Father refused to let him into the house. 'Isn't it enough that we got Reuben and a Spanish Catholic? Now we have Betty bringing home the schwartzes!' Looking back from the 1990s at Father's attitudes, it is easy to criticise him for being prejudiced but his outlook was not so different from many men of his generation, Jewish, Scots or whatever. In the end, something like tolerance began to affect him as he got used to Betty's coloured friends. He even stopped making jokes about golliwogs.

Eventually, I, little Hymie, was to experience the first stirrings of romance in my soul. The first person that I might describe as a girlfriend attended the Jewish school where I was sent for religious instruction. Even now, I'm sure she was beautiful. Her name was Ruby.

I was shy and totally inexperienced. Another handicap was a lack of friends to consult on matters amorous and erotic, but I was assisted by a boy called Sam. He was going around with Ruby's sister and helpfully suggested we make up a foursome.

I stumbled my way through the evening, feeling inept and dull. I could think of nothing to talk about. Then Sam whispered suddenly, 'You take yours home first,' and I was alone with Ruby, climbing the worn stairs of the tenement to her top flat home. We ascended in silence.

At her closed door we stood facing one another. We were breathing heavily, after the steep climb. Apart from that, the landing was silent as the grave, and shadowy. I remember her hair being outlined in the gloom but it was too dark to see her face. What was I to do? We stood for minutes, doing nothing. I was terrified of offending her. 'Is anything the matter?' she asked. 'You look a wee bit white.' I was frozen by indecision and couldn't even manage to answer the poor girl. The strain of my company then evidently became too much for Ruby. She burst into tears, then rushed into her house and slammed the door.

Miserably, I trailed down the stairs to meet Sam coming up with Ruby's sister. 'Ye've been quick,' he said, somewhat critically. I edged past them both, saying I'd wait for Sam outside. When Sam appeared again, he knew that Ruby had been crying. 'What did you say to upset her?' he asked.

'Nothing,' I replied with total honesty. Sam seemed much more of a man of the world than I was, and it was impossible to explain to him what had happened.

'Did you kiss her?' he persisted.

'No.'

'Huh!' he exclaimed. 'No wonder she's upset. You've missed your chance now.' Sam proceeded to find someone else to take Ruby out, having concluded that I was a dead loss. Every time I encountered Ruby I went through a hell of embarrassment. I certainly couldn't summon up the nerve to ask her out again. But the memory stayed with me, reminding me of my shyness, making me wary of trying to form relationships. For a while, I was friendly with a non-Jewish girl called Isa. She was cheery, with plenty to say. She was easy to be with – I didn't have to think up topics of conversation all the time. But I never felt strongly attracted to her, as I had to Ruby and, on the whole, I continued not to have much contact with the mysterious world of girls.

I was still a schoolboy when I met Ruby and Isa but I had been working for Father from the age of twelve. But I was now about to turn fourteen, which meant I would be officially grown-up and would be expected to start full-time work as soon as possible. I'd had my brief spell of secondary education at James Clark's School but there was never any thought of staying on to try for some qualifications. Fourteen was an important age for me, as it began the process of severance from my family, home and background.

At first, it was taken for granted that I would do whichever job

Father managed to find for me. I was never consulted. Career guidance was a concept which Father didn't trouble himself with. What happened was that at one of his masonic meetings, Father had a few words with a tailor and my destiny was decided, then and there. The following day I began work in the tailoring business.

There were a great many little tailoring concerns scattered all over our part of Edinburgh, very often run by Jews and employing Jews. There were individuals doing repairs in their kitchens and there were bigger firms, some of which survive in Edinburgh today. There were Jewish tailors, too, in Glasgow and in many of the big English cities. I was told that in the up-market areas of London, around Savile Row, customers would want their suits altered. The English assistant with the impeccable accent would note the requirements, then the suits would be delivered to back-street workshops where the poorly-paid Jewish tailors would do a first-class job. The point was that, in London, the Jews were kept out of sight; they were not to be seen anywhere as prestigious as Savile Row. But, as I've said, we didn't suffer from that kind of discrimination in our Happy Land in Edinburgh.

I may not have been discriminated against, but the place I worked in was an absolute sweat-shop. The address was impressive as it was in Hanover Street, just off Princes Street. However, we occupied the crowded top floor. Many of the men still worked in the old-fashioned position, sitting cross-legged on top of a table. It was a position I never felt comfortable in.

My duties were explained to me. They consisted of making tea and pressing sleeves in readiness for stitching. It was summer and my corner of the sweat-shop was next to the high, old-fashioned stove, because that was where the irons were. Perspiration poured down my face all day long. My clothes stuck to my body. I managed three months of tea-making and sleeve-pressing then walked out, never to return. I knew there had to be more to life.

I was old enough to be a working man, but I still lived in fear of my father. I couldn't tell him what I'd done, so every day I left home at the usual time. Instead of sweating over sleeves and tea, I would stroll among the exotic plants and trees of the Royal Botanic Garden. The peace and the beauty contrasted with the dark din of the tailor's premises, and the noise of my own home. I spent hours wandering and wondering what I could do to make my life pleasant. My period of introspection came to an abrupt end, however. Father went to another lodge meeting, spoke to his tailor friend and, next morning, the hellish belt swung into action again. The same day I left home.

I can recall hesitating on the dark stairway. I'd had enough of the overcrowding and the clamour. I'd certainly had enough of Father and his wild justice. But if he, at the time, seemed like a devil, then my mother was a protective angel from whose comforting warmth I was reluctant to tear myself away. I made my decision. I stepped out onto the pavement, positive that I would never cross the threshold again. I remember being almost overcome with depression, and feeling that I'd been pushed headlong into the world of adults. It seemed a cruel and unfair place.

But I didn't allow myself to wallow too long in self-pity. It had taken a lot of strength, at the age of fourteen, to walk out. I'd been brought up to be adaptable and self-sufficient. I would use these qualities to the limits. I realised there would be little time for idle daydreams but, already, positive plans were formulating in my mind. It had taken the hell of the sweat-shop and that last beating to knock me swiftly out of my childhood. With determination I picked up my bag and disappeared round the corner, away from St Leonard's Hill. I actually managed to whistle.

CHAPTER FOURTEEN

Looking Back, Moving Forward

My parents, brothers and sisters were not all that I left behind me that day. I was finally away from those chickens. Though my family couldn't afford to get sentimental over birds or beasts which could be cooked, we did love animals and sometimes kept pets. A short time after Father's hedgehog incident, he came from a fair in Inverness-shire with a sheepdog which we called Nairn. I don't know how many rings or watches he bartered for the dog, but he expected Kootky to be delighted with it. At first she was angry: 'Maurice Zoltie, don't we have enough mouths to fill?' She also expected that Nairn would add to the general din, but she soon softened and we all quickly grew to love the dog. We were therefore heartbroken when one day we couldn't find him anywhere. The police couldn't trace him and he wasn't at the cat and dog home. The house seemed miserably empty without him. We had to face the awful possibility that he'd had an accident.

A short time later a letter arrived for Father. It was post-marked Inverness-shire and came from the farmer who originally owned Nairn. Nairn was back at the farm. The dog must have walked from Edinburgh to Inverness-shire, a distance of more than one hundred and fifty miles. We were still sad but had to admire his spirit and intelligence.

Nairn was replaced by a big black cat. This pleased Mother immensely as it kept a close eye on the rats and mice which were regular visitors. We thought we had a tomcat until, one morning, we found five black kittens in a corner. Soon our cat was on a visit to the vet.

All cities seem to have their share of characters, the eccentrics who just don't seem to be out on the streets any more. Edinburgh was no exception. Near us, there was a woman known as Cattie Annie. Her speciality was rounding up stray (and not-so-stray) cats. She could often be seen walking large numbers of them on string leads. There was a rumour that she sold them for a shilling each to the dissectors at the university. We therefore kept a very careful watch on *our* feline friend. Motty unsettled us further by reporting a story he'd heard. It was said that Cattie Annie had been put out of business by a new Polish butcher who had opened up nearby. The locals muttered darkly among themselves, saying there was hardly a cat or a dog left to walk the streets. I'm sure the rumours were without foundation. We still hear similar tales today about ethnic restaurants. Anyway, our cat continued to live with us, adding to the mayhem of the house as she pursued her prey.

But, as I've said, at the ripe age of fourteen, I turned my back on them all, and left the nest. By that time it was 1928 and Reuben had married his Spanish girlfriend. The happy couple had a little flat of their own. They took me in and provided me with a temporary sanctuary where I could try to find some direction in my life. Having been, for years, one of a big group, I think I was desperate to assert myself as an individual. I would probably have said I was in search of self-expression, if I'd heard then of such a phrase. Of course, I lacked educational qualifications. It was bad enough leaving school at fourteen, but I'd also missed lessons through going to fairs and shows with Father – to sell balloons.

How was I to express myself? For some time I'd been surrounded by the trappings of photography. I'd seen Father and my brothers do quite well at it and I'd often watched professional photographers at work. That was it, I thought. I'd be a photographer.

It was suggested that I'd have to prove myself first as a freelance. So out I went and bought a box camera. I roamed the city in search of unusual subjects. I'd no wish to waste my talents on weddings or babies. Eventually I ended up at Granton, one of

Edinburgh's harbours. At that time, it was still a busy centre for fishing. My gaze came to rest on a steel hawser ring at the dock-side. I managed to balance it so that I could look through it, so that it acted like a circular frame. Then I sat down and waited until a passing trawler was in the right position and, click, I had the boat, framed in the circle of metal. I was pleased with the result – so pleased that, with amazing presumption, I sent it to the *Daily Express*. I was overjoyed when the picture was published, taking up nearly half a page. I bought twenty-four copies of the paper to make sure nobody missed my press debut. My confidence was boosted to the skies. How could I now fail?

I decided I would start my career on the local Edinburgh paper, the *Evening News*. I went along to the offices and demanded to see the art editor. The staff were probably so bemused that they just showed me in. I was brimming over with hope as I presented him with one of my copies of the *Daily Express*. He nodded at the photograph then asked me what else I'd done.

'Nothing,' I said, in all honesty.

He was astonished. 'Do you mean to say that this is the only picture you have?'

'Yes,' I confessed, feeling ever so slightly less sure of myself. I think he may have had some difficulty in stopping himself laughing, but he told me he would give consideration to any future pictures I might take.

My disappointment knew no bounds. I had naively hoped that, at the very least, I might become an apprentice photographer. Feeling downcast, I became painfully aware of my tousled hair and worn clothes. I still had a long way to go before I could call myself a success.

I decided to persevere with the photography. Well, I did have a camera, after all. I was tired, however, of tramping the streets, looking for interesting pictures. So I thought I would have a go at illustrating well-known proverbs. Soon I was seated in the public library with a dusty collection of proverbs open before me. 'He who laughs last, laughs best': I couldn't see *that* as a picture. 'An eye for an eye, a tooth for a tooth': that would be a tricky one. 'There's no use crying over spilt milk': now that seemed a possibility. My imagination began to whirr.

I approached a neighbour I knew who had a baby and a cat. She was happy enough to co-operate with me. We soon had the baby lying comfortably on some rugs on the floor. We took the baby's bottle and laid it on the floor beside a pool of milk. I wanted it to look as though the baby had dropped the bottle and the milk had spilt. The cat obligingly appeared to play its part, lapping up the pool of milk. All I needed to complete my pictorial proverb was the baby to cry. But the baby was happy. He just wanted to smile. Here was my creativity at stake and all he could do was lie there and grin! Desperate measures were required. I asked the mother to get me something from the kitchen and, while she was away, I quickly gave the baby a smack on the bottom. I know I was wrong. But the baby's face dissolved in tears and, click, I had my picture.

My dubious efforts were rewarded. The picture was published in a daily and a Sunday newspaper. I now felt I had some kind of track record. I was becoming established. Another of my compositions was used by a Dundee paper, in connection with Remembrance Day; but though I felt successful, the fees were not enough to live on.

I was wondering how I could improve my income when another photographer contacted me about an offer which, he said, was too good to refuse. It sounded an exciting proposition. If we worked together we could combine some lucrative employment with a holiday abroad. A cruise ship, the *Dunera*, was leaving Leith for a cruise of Scandinavia. Two photographers were required and there would be plenty of work available. I could be his assistant. I knew I was inexperienced but decided to take a chance in order to get away from the limited horizons of my Edinburgh upbringing. I became excited at the prospect.

We had to supply our own equipment and be paid on a

commission basis: the more pictures we took, the more we would earn, we assumed. There were about three hundred passengers and they seemed to be crammed into every square inch of space. We didn't have a proper dark room but we remained optimistic. We would manage somehow.

It was our job to photograph the special functions such as dances, fancy-dress balls and competitions. That was all straight-forward stuff but we discovered that it was also our duty to develop and print the films used by the passengers. And out of three hundred, there were a great many keen photographers. We were deluged with snapshots of funnels, seagulls and lop-sided studies of Auntie Morag at the captain's table. We couldn't cope. By the time we reached Copenhagen, we knew we would have to admit defeat. Jack, my fellow sufferer, was older and more experienced than I was but, even so, he was only about nineteen and had never been a cruise photographer before. Sitting despondently in our grotty cupboard of a cabin, we seemed a long way away from our dreams of exotic nightlife, strange food and pliant blonde beauties.

At Copenhagen we saw nothing. The passengers and crew went ashore while we slaved away with the films and chemicals. Another problem we discovered was that we couldn't work while the engine was running as the vibrations spoiled the pic-tures. Our processing had to be done while the ship was in dock. We worked round the clock and emerged from our cabin for a breath of air. We were in time to see the return of the passengers, laden with undeveloped views of Copenhagen.

We decided to mutiny. What was the point of being in Scan-dinavia and seeing nothing? So, at the next port of call we mingled with the camera-toting hordes and slipped ashore. I remember a nightclub and some girls who were, very obviously, after what little money we had. We were soon thoroughly drunk, but managed to lurch into a taxi and get back on board before the ship sailed at midnight.

We told each other that it would be quite acceptable for us to catch up with the huge backlog of film when we returned to Edinburgh. No one would mind, we assured one another. We became more and more like passengers, except for photographing the occasional dance. Whenever we docked, we had a night on the town.

All this carefree living was fine until one night, after several drinks on shore, I got separated from Jack. I assumed he would have enough sense to make his own way back to the *Dunera* so I returned alone. The ship sailed in the small hours with still no sign of Jack. Oh well, I told myself, he's probably got himself into a cabin with some ravishing beauty. He'll tell me about it in the morning.

But he didn't, because he was missing. I reported this anxiously to one of the ship's officers and a search was mounted. Jack couldn't be found. I was hauled up for questioning. Had my friend shown signs of depression? I suppose they were wondering if he might have thrown himself into the Baltic in despair. I told them what I knew but it wasn't much help.

The mystery was solved shortly afterwards when the captain received notification from the British Consul. Jack, after his night of merry-making, had merely missed the boat. We had to make a special trip to Oslo on our return journey, just to rescue Jack. Naturally, the captain was furious about the inconvenience. We had to admit that the work was too much for us and we had no experience as cruise photographers. This meant that my next position was a lowly one – on the ship's crew. We spent the rest of the trip doing menial chores, including scrubbing the decks. It was a huge relief to step once more onto dry Scottish land.

The *Dunera* episode should have taught me a lesson. But, in a way, it summed up the way I was to go through life. I continued to take chances if I thought there was any hope of rich rewards or good experience. I also continued to get my fingers burnt when things didn't turn out quite as I'd anticipated.

CHAPTER FIFTEEN

Searching

I've never found it easy just to sit and work in one place. I definitely inherited some of my father's wanderlust. My next venture had me touring village fairs in an old car. I managed to scrape together the money to buy it, but I was pretty hard up.

My idea was to rip out the back seats and improvise a small dark-room, so that I would have my very own travelling business premises. I planned to take photographs and then, within an hour, produce proofs and take orders actually at the fair. It worked well, presumably because I'd devised a method that none of my competitors had thought of.

There were, inevitably, drawbacks. The car was quite cramped. If I had a lot of orders, I'd often have to work late at night. On one such night, at about 1 am, I was parked in a side street and, in a crouched position, was busy at work with my enlarger. But the policeman who happened to wander past didn't assume that the car was a photographer's dark-room. It was dark deeds that he thought of. A private car, at night, with blacked-out windows and strange noises coming from within, could only mean one thing. It must have seemed straight from the pages of *The News Of The World*.

He rapped sharply on one of the doors, possibly expecting to cause a panic. 'Come out of there!' he ordered, probably wondering about what manner of depraved behaviour he'd uncovered. I did panic. I was terrified that he'd open the door and let light get at the plate I was working on. I hung onto the door, thus confirming his suspicions. He began to tug from the outside while I hung on desperately with all my strength.

'Come on! What are you up to in there?' he growled.

'I'm developing photographs,' I shouted back. A highly

unlikely story in the circumstances, I have to admit. I won the struggle and managed to save the plate. Then I let him yank the door open. His face fell when he saw I was alone and there was no ripe catch for him. He went away, shaking his head in disbelief.

I steadily built up my business by doing routine work such as weddings, christenings and dances. I got my own little studios, first in South Bridge then in Castle Street. As the years went by the relationship between Reuben and his wife Lola became strained to breaking point. The fighting and the noise reminded me of home so I moved away from them and found myself struggling to get by, often eating little more than bread and soup or some cheap fish. By the time I was nineteen, I was thoroughly wearied of my existence. It had become humdrum and I was sick of the endless canvassing for work. My heart leapt with excitement, therefore, when my phone rang and I was offered some unusual work – at the airport. A commercial company was wanting some aerial photographs. 'Are you experienced in aerial photography?' asked the voice.

'Oh, of course,' I lied. The next day I was at Turnhouse Airport with my camera.

Having never been up in a plane before, I was trembling with excitement and apprehension as I climbed into the seat behind the pilot. He explained to me that he would point down with his forefinger when we were over certain places that were to be photographed. That sounded easy enough until we shuddered into motion and roared into the air. My stomach was churning. The landscape lurched and tilted below us. I sat scarcely daring to breathe in case I knocked the plane off course. Then it happened. The forefinger pointed. I forced myself to peek cautiously over the side and, with trembling hands, pointed my camera hopefully downward. The pilot, trying to be helpful, tilted the plane. My immediate thought was that, in spite of my harness, I was being emptied out of the plane. Instinctively, I grabbed the edge of my seat. Before I realised what I'd done, my treasured camera was spinning through the air.

86

The pilot was busy with the controls and had no notion of the disastrous events taking place behind his back. We continued to circle and, every so often, he would point his forefinger downward as I sat there uselessly looking about me, a photographer without a camera. I was too ashamed to speak.

At last we landed and the pilot asked breezily, 'Got some good shots, son?' Silently, I climbed out. 'Where's your camera?' he asked, looking at me with growing suspicion. We made our way into the office. Recriminations flew back and forward. The representative from the company tried to blame me for having no experience. And who was going to pay for the wasted plane hire?

I was dispirited, but I fought back the best I could. 'What about my camera?' I demanded. Needless to say, it wasn't insured and represented my entire livelihood. The company threatened to sue me for inefficiency so I threatened to sue them for having caused me to lose my camera. We parted bitterly.

With barely enough money to scrape by, I was now desperate. I was also lonely. I couldn't afford even to go to a dance in the hope of meeting someone. I'd never managed to leave behind the sense of isolation that had so often haunted me as a child. That was why, I suppose, I'd developed a habit of browsing through the personal columns of newspapers and magazines. One day a reference to pen-friends caught my eye. It made me realise that I wasn't the only person who was lonely. There were undoubtedly thousands of people who felt isolated. But my solution wasn't to get myself a pen-friend. I decided I could solve both my financial and my personal problems by starting a bureau to bring people together.

As with all my new ideas, it took me over. Here was a fresh enterprise, a challenge. I borrowed some capital from one of my brothers, rented an office and launched the Margaret Morrison Scottish Pen-friendship Club. Who was Margaret Morrison? The answer is, she didn't exist. I just thought that a woman's name would give the club's name more of a suggestion of sympathy and understanding.

I advertised the club in several countries, including America, Switzerland and India. I then placed advertisements in Scottish magazines, claiming I had members all over the world. The membership fee was five shillings or its equivalent in foreign currency. I waited for the sackfuls of mail but either there were fewer lonely people than I had anticipated or my idea wasn't appealing enough. Response was sluggish. My despondency began to settle around me like a heavy cloud.

One morning I was sitting waiting for the postman when there was a brisk knock at the door. I was pleasantly surprised to find it was a man I'd never met before. I innocently assumed he was lonely and wanted a pen-pal. I welcomed him but my enthusiasm turned to alarm when he revealed the true purpose of his visit. He was a newspaper reporter. It seemed that one of my clients, a Glasgow masseur, had met his pen-friend and been so delighted with her that they were getting married. It was a perfect newspaper romance and so the reporter wanted an interview with Margaret Morrison.

'Is she here at the moment?' he asked, peering around my small office. He obviously assumed I was some kind of lackey who worked for the great lady.

'Er, no. Not at the moment,' I replied with conviction.

'Well, can I make an appointment? Perhaps later in the day,' he persisted, getting out his notebook.

'Well, no,' I said, evasively. 'Actually, she's away in London on business.'

The reporter looked disappointed. He could see his story slipping from his grasp. I thought quickly. An article in the press about my club could only be beneficial. 'She should be back tomorrow,' I announced decisively. He brightened visibly, but what was I going to do about Margaret Morrison? I could hardly dress up in drag.

I concluded that my only possible course of action was to persuade someone to impersonate her. I used to say good-morning to a typist in the office next to mine. After some pleading, she agreed to help me out of my predicament, so long as it didn't take up more than half an hour of her time. She either felt sorry for me or thought I was eccentric and ought to be humoured. I gave her the basic details and to my relief she carried the whole thing off successfully. The reporter went away happily with his story.

Shortly afterwards, an envelope arrived from Glasgow. It was addressed to Margaret Morrison and was an invitation to the well-publicised wedding of my client and his bride-to-be. I hopefully approached the typist in the next office. I even took her some flowers, but she refused to go to the wedding as Margaret Morrison.

After my little flurry of publicity I received one or two inquiries, but soon the mail reduced to a trickle then stopped completely. My idea had flopped but I could console myself with the thought that I'd made at least two people happy.

Once again I was left feeling alone and directionless. It was years since I'd seen my parents, and I'd grown to regret the gulf which cut me off from home. I met my sister Anna who suggested a compromise: I should visit Mother while Father was out at work. As I had no argument with my mother, Anna's proposal seemed sensible.

I thought I might feel odd, back at St Leonard's Hill; I expected to feel as if I didn't belong but, when I got there, I was aware of nothing but a warm glow of affection. I felt protected again.

It was a relief to have healed, at least partially, the rift with my parents. I was, however, still jobless. I decided I needed to start a completely new life. I'd follow my father's two brothers to the land of opportunity. I'd head for America!

CHAPTER SIXTEEN

My War

The Jews have been a wandering people throughout their history. My father, after coming all the way to Edinburgh from Bialystok, could never settle down to work at one thing in one place. I seemed condemned to follow in the tradition. In desperation I wrote to my uncle in Chicago, convinced that there would be more opportunities for me in the vastness of the USA. Eventually, I got all the arrangements completed but was told there would be a waiting period of two months before I could sail from Glasgow. I was to leave on 1 September. The year was 1939.

My excitement mounted; the ticket finally arrived. Then, with only one week to go before my departure for the New World, a letter came from the company stating simply that all the shipping had been cancelled due to the threat of war. I stood holding the flimsy sheet of paper, barely able to believe that it represented the end of all my plans, my new dreams.

On 1 September, instead of my leaving for America, Hitler invaded Poland and caused my own little drama to pale into insignificance. I was soon caught up in the wave of patriotic fervour which swept Britain. My immediate future was decided for me. I would join the RAF, even though I was not yet due to be called up for military service.

I went to the recruiting office where a smart officer with the appropriate handlebar moustache faced me across a table. I told him I was a press photographer and that I could type. I thought he'd be very impressed by these abilities.

'Have you ever been up in a plane?' he inquired.

'Oh yes,' I replied, truthfully enough. 'I've been up in a plane to take photographs.' Momentarily, I had a vision of my camera spinning through space.

The officer's eyebrows shot up. He told me there was a big demand for men to take reconnaissance photographs. He asked me what my flying time was. That was a tricky question. My answer was very vague and non-committal. Nevertheless, the officer still seemed keen and asked me to come back the following day. I imagined myself swaggering down the street in a smart uniform decorated with wings and medals. 'I'm in aerial reconnaissance,' I would tell all the girls. 'Very important work.' At that time, nobody had told me that there was a big demand for airborne photographers as there was a particularly big mortality rate among them.

The next day I returned to the recruiting office for more questions. I was twenty-five. Fine. I was Scottish. Fine. But what about my father? A Russian? And a Dutch mother with a trace of German? I could see the interest in me draining from the officer's face as I sat there. He told me that I wasn't eligible for reconnaissance flying as my father had never been naturalised. Perhaps, he suggested, I would like to try the Army.

I left the office in a fury. I'd been ready and willing to serve the land of my birth and I'd been turned down for what seemed the flimsiest of reasons. All right. They could keep their planes for themselves. I immediately applied to join the Royal Army Ordinance Corps. I was accepted.

On my way out of the office, I found myself chatting with another new recruit. I told him I'd joined the Ordinance Corps. He told me I was a bloody fool; I should have joined the Royal Army Service Corps as they served behind the lines. So impressionable was I that I went straight back into the office and said I'd changed my mind. I wasn't popular that day and I'm sorry to admit that my career in the Army was to continue along similar lines.

Eventually I was given my medical and presented with two shillings. 'What's this?' I asked naively.

'A day's pay,' was the reply. 'After all, you get your food and uniform for nothing.'

Before very long I found myself at Portsmouth being trained. I'd left St Leonard's Hill because of the overcrowding, the mass of bodies, the noise and my father's severe discipline. And here I now was, being yelled at and sharing a hut with twenty-nine other men. I knew that Hitler was rampaging across Europe but I couldn't help feeling I'd been an idiot to volunteer for endless parading up and down a barrack square with a gun on my shoulder. I grew to hate all the NCOs. I was convinced they had a spite against me, though in fact they treated all the men the same. Dreadfully.

The Army rules and regulations forbade any form of trading but I was blissfully ignorant of the fact; at least at first. It was popular among the men to wear cap badges. The theory was that these badges were supplied free by the Army; in actual fact they had to be bought at a local Army and Navy Store. My entrepreneurial instincts led me to write to the badge manufacturers and obtain a large supply. The barber then sold these for me, getting his due commission in the process. Encouraged by the success of this little venture, I organised raffles. For a threepenny ticket, a soldier had the chance of winning fifty cigarettes. The raffles were popular and brought me nearly one hundred per cent profit. Well, I *was* only being paid two shillings a day.

Despite my little enterprises, I found it difficult to make any real friends. Nowadays I can accept that I am, by nature, a loner; then, as a young man, my isolation worried and depressed me. I became more and more disillusioned with Army routine. One day, I wandered all over the town and forgot to turn up for duty at the barracks. As a result, I was put on a charge. I became so fed up with it all that I could see only one possible answer. I would have to run away; in a word, desert. I began to plan my escape as though I were a POW.

I considered buying a second-hand suit, changing in a public toilet and making straight for the railway station. But I was too terrified of being flung into prison. So I continued for a time as I was: a very unhappy misfit.

The one treat I used to enjoy was frequenting a rather expensive restaurant in Portsmouth. I still had my enthusiasm for good food. The establishment was, however, usually used by officers and some eyebrows were raised at my humble presence. I was asked how I could afford the prices on my low pay. I tried to pass it off airily with vague comments about there being money in the family. My St Leonard's origins must have been all too obvious because nobody believed my tales. It was then discovered that my gourmet excursions were financed by an illicit trade in cap badges. It was interrogation time.

I suppose I was lucky. I got off with a severe reprimand and was transferred, away from my business interests, to Southampton. Unfortunately, I didn't know a soul there and became even more isolated. I was put in a bleak little office and given clerical duties relating to the embarkation of troops. Sitting at my desk reminded me of being back at school. I didn't like it.

People, nowadays, sometimes think I'm rather a bleak-looking character. I think my general mien might stem from these army days on the south coast. It all became a vicious circle: I looked miserable as I didn't have friends and people didn't attempt to befriend me as I looked so miserable. Also, at the time, I began to believe that my Jewish appearance didn't help matters.

Remembering the fictitious Margaret Morrison, I cheered myself up a little by joining a pen-pal club and sending off pages of my troubles to a sympathetic lady. I made very good use of the office typewriter. I produced a pile of short articles on various subjects and posted them off to magazines but they were never published. However, it all helped to keep me busy and prevented me from dwelling on myself. I got so involved with my literary endeavours that I used to stay late at the office, just to use the typewriter.

In any wartime situation, the authorities are always on the look-out for anyone who might be spreading subversive propaganda. At that time, there was a scare about fifth-columnists being dropped into the country by parachute. And there was I, a loner with a foreign appearance, spending endless unpaid hours at the typewriter. What on earth was I up to? It was interrogation time again.

I was marched off under open arrest and taken to HQ where about a dozen Intelligence Officers were waiting to question me. It seemed I'd been under surveillance for some time. And now they'd caught me red-handed – typing letters to my pen-pal.

There were three lines of questioning. I was asked, naturally, about all my after-hours typing. I told them the truth, though even to me my story sounded a bit lame. I began to imagine a court martial. I'd been observed having conversations around town; I'd been overheard asking other soldiers where they were stationed. 'Explain that if you can,' I was asked. My perfectly innocent, casual conversations were being interpreted in the most sinister light. The officers clearly suspected me of gathering information to send off to Germany. It seemed utterly ridiculous to me. I'd rushed out to volunteer to help to fight Hitler. How could I be a traitor? *And* I was a Jew!

'Why,' I was asked, 'do you masquerade as an officer in the street?' I was baffled at first by that one. Then I remembered that the rough material of my battledress had caused a rash to break out on my neck and I'd worn a collar and tie for a couple of days to allow it to heal. I explained this to the officers.

There was much deliberation as I stood, like an accused murderer, awaiting the verdict. In the end, they appeared to believe me and I was dismissed from the room. I was still, however, regarded as a somewhat dubious character. Why else would I be removed from my Army typewriter and put on a range of lowly duties which included cleaning the lavatories? Another hated duty to which I was assigned was clearing away rubble after air-raids, to uncover bodies, alive and dead.

My Army career was not a success. I just didn't fit in. Whatever I did seemed to get me into trouble. More and more, I found myself considering desertion. I discovered I was not alone in having such an ambition. A new man, Sammy Cohen, arrived at our unit. His theory was that if he convinced the authorities he was deranged, he would be put out of the Army as unfit. So he turned up for parade one morning with his rifle upside down and his hat on side-ways in the style of Napoleon. The sergeant dismissed him and he duly disappeared. I assumed Sammy had been successful but I didn't much relish the idea of pretending to be mad. As it was, I already aroused quite enough suspicion.

And as it turned out, there was no need for me to feign insanity. Although I hadn't recognised the fact, I'd been under considerable stress for some time. An increase in the air-raids made my condition worse and, without requesting it, I was put into hospital for rest and observation. After a few weeks, I returned to my duties only to experience a relapse; on the verge of a breakdown, I saw doctors and a psychiatrist and was sent back to hospital, this time in Sutton, near London. This did little to reassure me as, one day, just after lunch, part of the hospital was blown up by a bomb. I was soon on the move again, this time westwards, and ended up in Somerset, in a hospital which at one time had been for mental patients.

I was interviewed by a psychiatrist again. He seemed to be trying to find out why I couldn't fit in with Army life. He was trained to detect malingerers but recognised that I was genuinely emotionally ill. In our conversations he discovered that I had a familiarity with the German language, via my parents' Yiddish. This gave him an idea. He concluded that it was perhaps the boredom of Army routine that was getting me down. I needed excitement and a challenge. I think he was right, but I wasn't over-enthusiastic about the remedy he suggested. He offered to get me on a course to improve my German, after which I could join a parachute regiment and, eventually, work as an agent in occupied Europe. Why, I wondered, did everyone insist in regarding me as a possible spy?

I thanked him for his suggestion but explained that being dropped by parachute behind enemy lines didn't really appeal to me all that much. On reflection, the boredom seemed preferable.

95

The psychiatrist did his best for me but came to the conclusion that I was just emotionally unsuited to military life. I was discharged from the Army.

CHAPTER SEVENTEEN

Developing

It was 1941 and the war was getting worse when I returned as a civilian to Edinburgh. Everywhere there were young men in khaki to make me feel conspicuous, the odd one out. I needed a job, quickly.

I was taken on by a firm of photographers in Glasgow. There was a boom in photography at the time and they had several branch studios around the country. After six months they offered to make me their manager in York. I jumped at the chance; there was little to keep me in Scotland. Delighted as I was to get the York job, it did feel a little unusual to be working for someone else. In the past, I'd nearly always been my own boss. That was also to be the case in the future.

There was no end to the work in York. Servicemen were keen to be photographed in their uniforms and often there were queues down the street. Soon, however, I was itching for a change of scene and the firm obligingly sent me to its Huddersfield branch where my pay was increased. It was there that I was able to fix myself up with my very own bachelor flat. At last I had some peace and freedom. I saved enough money to be able to part company with the Glasgow firm, then got back into business for myself. I knew there was plenty of work available. I rented premises in the fun-fair in Manchester's Oldham Street. I had a booth where I took orders, and upstairs I had a small, basic studio. I had little else besides a 35mm camera and an enlarger which I'd bought second-hand. But I did all right. It only took a few weeks to be able to afford more equipment and take on two employees. The queues appeared every day and soon I was thinking of opening up in a proper shop.

Someone told me about an empty shop in Sheffield city centre.

It became my new photographic studio. Making money was almost effortless; it seemed I couldn't fail. I even went back to Edinburgh and visited my father. He seemed pleased that I was finally being successful financially.

I opened up studios in Barnsley, Stoke-on-Trent, Hanley, Warrington and Edinburgh. The processing work was centralised in Manchester. At last, I had more money than I needed but I soon found that it didn't bring me the satisfaction I sought. I was still restless. My life seemed incomplete.

Still, I persevered in my new role as a successful businessman. My Warrington branch, I discovered, was particularly well situated. Americans were stationed nearby and they seemed to have an insatiable appetite for pictures of themselves. However, one busy morning a detective arrived at the shop. 'Are you aware, sir,' he began, 'that your studio has been placed out of bounds to American troops?' I was dumbfounded. I'd heard of pubs and clubs being out of bounds but what was wrong with an innocent 'snap'? The detective explained that some Americans had been seen going into the shop after hours. I knew nothing about that and could only conclude that my manageress was doing extra photographic work without my knowledge and making a bit on the side, at my expense. The detective smiled, the way he might have smiled at a little boy who didn't quite understand what was going on.

'I think, sir,' he explained, 'that the men are coming round for more than a quick picture.' Belatedly, I got the message. I could see the headlines in the Sunday papers: PHOTOGRAPHER'S STUDIO OF SIN or YANKEE TROOPS GET THE PICTURE IN WARRINGTON LOVE NEST. After that, the studio was locked and shuttered at tea-time and I carried the only keys. If my manageress was upset by her drop in income, she didn't let me know.

Some of the emptiness which I'd been aware of in my life was relieved when, in Manchester, I employed a photographic re-toucher called Joan. She was a very attractive red-head with bright blue eyes. I liked her manner, which was rather hesitant. She seemed very sensitive. We became close friends. I knew there were whole worlds of experience of which I was ignorant and I was ready to learn. Joan was the person to teach me. She knew about politics, religion and philosophy and this resulted in our having endless debates into the small hours. She came from Liverpool, where she'd been associated with the Communist Party. This made us, in some ways, an odd couple, as she saw me as a typical capitalist intent on expanding my photographic empire. And she disapproved. She truly believed that spiritual attainments were much more important than a big bank account. She was to alter my whole approach to life.

Through her, I met people of a sort I'd never encountered before. She had a wide circle of friends: the owner of an Indian restaurant, a writer, university students. All of them seemed incredibly cultured and intelligent. When we met at first I was almost afraid to open my mouth in case I seemed an inarticulate imbecile. But they were friendly people and encouraged me to come out of my shell. I felt a deep sense of relief. It was as though a tap had been turned on and everything that had been dammed up inside my mind for years was finally allowed out.

I became painfully aware of the gaps in my education but, encouraged by Joan, I enrolled for a course of extramural studies at Manchester University. It made me realise that though my upbringing had been loving, the insistence on upholding the Jewish faith and the narrow concentration on events within the family had had a very restricting effect. There had been little encouragement to broaden out or even be aware of other ideas.

John lived surrounded by ideas in a flat which resembled a second-hand bookshop. Newspapers and magazines were piled on the furniture and floor. There was barely room for her bed. I enjoyed the contrast between my business interests and the company of Joan and her friends.

As my relationship with my parents had improved, they decided to come down to Manchester and visit their successful

99

boy. I usually had to work at least until tea-time but Joan
volunteered to entertain them until I arrived. When I got home
they were all seated at the table. After greeting my parents, I
asked if they'd enjoyed their tea.

'Oh yes,' said Father.

'What did you have?' I asked.

'Ham and eggs,' he replied laughingly.

'Did you enjoy it?' I enquired with some surprise.

'It was lovely,' he exclaimed with a big grin. When Mother
nudged him in the ribs I realised he was joking. Joan had cooked
them ham and eggs but the meal had been politely refused. She'd
had no idea how strictly the laws about unkosher food were
observed. Father's visit must have brought home to him just how
far his son had moved away from his Jewish roots. He never
forgot his plate of ham and eggs and still mentioned it years later,
regarding it as a great joke.

My friendship with Joan continued, on and off, for some years
but my initial enthusiasm cooled. She could never really accept
my need to make a profit all the time. At one point she even tried
to talk me into leaving it all behind and becoming a warden in a
youth hostel or working for the Forestry Commission. Whatever
I might have thought of my father, there was little doubt that his
business sense had been well and truly instilled in me. I was stuck
with it.

Though I made a living for many years at photography, I lost
interest in the routine and was always keen to experiment with
any new venture. After getting into a fix (just like Father) over
some cheap photographic paper I'd purchased which turned out
to be black-market, I was keen for some kind of change.

One day, while strolling through Manchester, I stopped to
look at a Government Surplus clothing shop. Such shops were,
naturally, thriving at the time, selling boots and socks, shirts and
blankets. A bonus was that clothing coupons weren't required to
buy the goods. I made up my mind to turn one of my studios into
such a store. There I was again, allowing a novelty to take me over.

I bought a selection of suitable goods but delighted myself most with the purchase I regarded as my *pièce de résistance*. I was convinced that one of my most popular lines would be two thousand pairs of WAAF knickers with elasticated legs. What a scoop! I advertised them at a shilling a pair but was disheartened to find that the front door wasn't broken down in the rush. Women were managing to resist the allure of these sensible garments. Never mind; I could sell them at sixpence a pair and still do well on the deal. But still no frantic bargain hunters appeared on the horizon. Finally, I had to let the knickers go at threepence a pair, just to get rid of them. My enthusiasm had been curbed.

Boots and trousers were a nightmare. There were so many men coming into the shop that I found it impossible to keep every size and length in stock. After lengthy haggling with a tailor in the city's Jewish quarter, I came to an arrangement about alterations and I was able to increase my trouser sales.

After about nine months of Government Surplus trading I was unpleasantly surprised to discover how low the profits were. It's always been my way to concentrate on expanding my business ventures and I've never spent much energy on accounts. This has always meant that I've been an easy target for any less than scrupulous staff. Such a staff member had been regularly pocketing my profits throughout the nine months. We parted company, swiftly.

I persevered, still hoping to make a reasonable success out of the surplus clothing, and took on a new and trustworthy manageress. I bought quantities of goods direct from the Government's own sales department auctions. I thought this would simplify matters but, as I ought to have known, nothing is ever straightforward. I soon discovered that there was a 'ring' of traders who had come to an aggreement not to bid against one another. My natural inclination was to go it alone but at the back of my mind I had a vague fear of American-style rackets. It seemed wisest just to comply with the 'ring' and avoid rocking the boat.

Government Surplus must be one of the least glamorous types of goods with which to be involved. In fact, it is difficult to think of anything much duller than those fusty piles of blankets or, for that matter, my mountainous heap of elasticated knickers. I soon grew tired of it all. I think part of the disillusionment stemmed from the fact that it reminded me too much of Father's early struggles to sell clothes from his packs. I suppose I liked to think I'd left all that behind me.

In all my various experiments, there was usually one final straw which broke this camel's back. Oddly enough, it was photographic film which finished me with Government Surplus. Once again, it seemed like a bargain not to be missed.

A large stock of surplus film came my way and I reckoned it could be cut up, packaged and sold cheaply as 120mm rolls. The work had to be done in a dark room and I hired women to tackle the work. It was very fast film and it occurred to me that its original purpose might have been for aerial reconnaissance. I was pleased to think that it was going to be used for peacetime entertainment rather than to help pinpoint targets for bombers.

The film sold well but, after a few weeks, the complaints began to arrive. I checked the film and found the whole lot faulty. Any photograph taken had a foggy patch on it. So another venture quietly died, leaving me jaded and depressed. When I'd first arrived in Manchester, I'd found it vital and exciting. It was a place where business seemed to thrive and things could happen. Eventually, it just seemed big, noisy and grimy. I'd had enough.

An acquaintance, noting how bleak I looked, suggested I should go along to the Ulmann School of Dancing. I'd already had a taste of psychoanalysis but my visit to the dancing school started me off on a lifelong series of experiments with almost every kind of therapy imaginable. I'd already spent a lot of my time experimenting in my work. I realised I now had to devote time to learning how to unwind and relax.

Free expression was the order of the day at the Ulmann School. So while wild Indian and African music surged from a record player, I joined the other strained executives as they flung their arms about and gyrated themselves into trances. With my eyes closed and my body writhing, I found myself hoping that no one I knew would see me in my abandoned state.

The dancing was enjoyable enough. It relaxed me temporarily but did not, I'm afraid, cure my malaise. I felt like a run-down motor in need of an overhaul. I closed down some studios; I'd lost interest. I stayed in the Manchester area, centring my remaining photographic interests in Didsbury where my staff was reduced to two. I would soon be on the move again. To America.

CHAPTER EIGHTEEN

My Tartan Dream

Ever since 1939, I'd felt disappointed about missing out on my proposed trip to the United States. It occurred to me that, now the war was over, an excursion across the Atlantic might be the answer to my problems. I was still living in England but made occasional trips back to Edinburgh where the green hills, open squares and rows of Georgian buildings always refreshed me after the industrial gloom of Manchester. I was able to see Edinburgh with new eyes, having been away from it for some years, and a new scheme began to form in my mind. Though my Russian, Dutch, German and Jewish heritage hardly qualified me as a true Scot, it did help me to see Scotland from the point of view of an outsider. And I'd long realised the great, almost mystical, attraction Scotland has for foreigners, especially Americans and Canadians.

The end of the war saw an end to the great demand for photographs. Gradually, I wound up the business and turned my attention to my new venture. At the time, the Board of Trade was very keen to encourage any form of export which might bring dollars into beleaguered Britain, so it was possible to get official backing for any reasonable-sounding scheme. My plan, quite simply, was to sell Scottish ancestry to the Americans. By mail order, I would give them the opportunity of buying goods in their own family tartans, direct from Scotland. The potential market was vast but first I had to do some research. I wasn't too sure about what kind of merchandise to deal in but I was already imagining a healthy trade in wooden heraldic shields or tartan neckties. Anything, in fact, that would allow a Mr Campbell or MacGregor in San Francisco or Seattle to say, 'I'm a Scot and this here is my tartan!' I foresaw an advertising slogan along the lines of, 'Be Proud Of Your Heritage.' But first, if I was to run a mail order business, I had to find out where all the Scots and their descendants actually lived in America.

My first trip was to the American Consulate in Edinburgh. They suggested that I contact the various clan societies which exist in North America. I was a little wary of this line of approach as I thought they might not look too kindly on what was an obviously commercial venture being promoted by someone of Russian, German, Dutch and Jewish origins, even if I was born in Scotland's capital. I would try a more direct approach.

I spent long hours in an Edinburgh public library, scanning the New York telephone directory, the only American one available at the time. I searched through all the German, Polish, Spanish, Italian and Jewish names for anything that sounded remotely Scottish. There were of course, many Macs but I began to wonder about the wisdom of trying to sell to New Yorkers. Would they not be too cynical and worldly-wise? I really needed names and addresses in small towns where I imagined the people would be less sophisticated.

Still filled with enthusiasm, I took a train to London and to the American Consulate there. They were surprisingly helpful and sat me at a desk with a telephone directory for each American state. After several days of eye-straining dedication, I had collected the names of some five thousand unsuspecting American citizens, scattered throughout the United States. I was glad to get this chore over; not only was it tiresome but I was beginning to be looked at suspiciously by the consulate staff. Obviously, they weren't entrepreneurs.

I returned to Edinburgh. I had my names and addresses; the next task was to stir up an interest in tartan goods. I decided to produce a sprat to catch a mackerel. My initial approach would be to send out five thousand letters advertising personalised tartan scrolls for a dollar each. Each scroll, complete with its own genuine red wax seal, would prove the owner's Scottish ancestry and clan membership. Once I'd sold the relatively cheap scrolls, my plan was to send a catalogue of more expensive tartan goods. Then, I hoped, I'd be in business.

My initial letters couldn't be on any old notepaper. I had to have Scottish paper. Finding paper with tartan edges wasn't easy but I managed eventually and had it headed with an illustration of a plane flying over Edinburgh Castle, en route for the New World. As well as my own address the paper bore the slogan: DIRECT FROM THE SCOTTISH CAPITAL TO YOUR HOME. I felt confident I'd stumbled upon a winning idea.

My next concern was the number of personalised scrolls I would need. I was optimistic but knew I wasn't going to get five thousand orders. I settled for a thousand scrolls. As well as the red seal, each would display a map of Scotland and a potted history of the appropriate clan. The scroll would look like parchment and, as a bonus, there would be a specimen of the clan tartan. But there was a snag. There are about one hundred and twenty different tartans and I had no way of knowing what would be the demand for each. The Mackays might turn out to be a highly emotional and patriotic lot and flood me with orders; on the other hand, one of the other clans might be a dour, canny bunch and order none at all. All I could do was plunge in and order a thousand assorted scrolls and hope for the best. I could put in a further order if necessary.

I enjoyed the excitement of my project, especially as it was going to involve me in a trip to America. First, however, I had to make inquiries about the availability of tartan goods for my proposed catalogue. At times, I felt the whole business was verging on the absurd, but somehow I enjoyed it all the more for that. It was an improvement on dealing in army boots and blankets.

I contacted wholesale manufacturers of tartan shirts, ties, scarves, socks, handkerchiefs, dressing-gowns and travelling-rugs. I wanted to find firms which would be able to meet my big orders quickly. I'd heard accounts of foreigners being irritated by British companies failing to meet delivery dates. I told the manufacturers that it would probably be necessary for their employees to work overtime when my orders eventually came through. I went so far as to contact 'reserve' manufacturers in Glasgow and Fife, in case my main suppliers were unable to cope with the rush. I made inquiries about having a lavishly illustrated catalogue produced but decided that, at that stage, I couldn't afford the cost. That would have to come when the dollars were pouring in.

At last I felt secure enough to despatch my tartan letters across the Atlantic. As well as the cost of the stationery and the scrolls, I landed myself with a £125 bill for stamps. Still, I assured myself, it would be money well invested. I thought back to my dark days in Manchester when the newspaper headlines had branded me as a blackmarket photographer. Changed days now, I thought proudly. I was doing my bit to encourage the export drive and help my country. I couldn't wait for my tartan dreams to come true.

My letters were all signed with the name Donald Stewart; it suggested hills and heather just a wee bit more than Zoltie did. I could see Donald in my mind's eye: he was a big strapping chap in a kilt. And he never went anywhere without his bagpipes. But what if one of my future American customers were to arrive in Edinburgh on holiday and decide to look up Donald? Instead of a sturdy Highlander there would be a rather swarthy businessman whose foreign features certainly didn't suggest a boyhood in the glens. Still, I'd already coped with a similar situation when I found a substitute for Margaret Morrison, the pen-pals' friend. If the worst came to the worst, I'd hire a suitable (or kiltable) Scotsman and call him Donald for the day.

The tense waiting for replies began. Ten days passed. I began to get anxious. I'd never had any dealings with America before and didn't realise how long the mail could take. I phoned the GPO to ask them to account for the delay. Everything was functioning normally, I was assured. The relief was enormous when, at last, five letters with American postmarks came through my letter-box. This was the trickle before the avalanche, I decided.

With trembling hands I opened the envelopes. The first person wanted to know if I could trace his great, great grandmother who'd lived, he thought, somewhere near Inverness. The second wanted pen-friends living in and around Edinburgh. But the other three actually wanted parchment scrolls. This so excited me that I considered putting in an order for an extra thousand, but caution prevailed and I told myself to wait a little longer.

Two more days passed; no letters. The third day produced a haul of one. Had I blundered? A nasty unease began to creep through me. I opened the single envelope. A dollar was enclosed with an order for a scroll. But there was a problem. The sender was called Anderson and he wanted to belong to a clan. But he was black. It was so absurd I couldn't help laughing. Nevertheless, he got his scroll and I like to think of him proudly displaying it on the wall of his living-room in St Louis. A cowboy wrote to me from Wyoming. As far as he knew, he didn't have a drop of Scottish blood but would be pleased if I could trace some Scottish ancestors for him. He didn't order a scroll.

This handful of replies seemed a disappointing response to my five thousand letters. I began to suspect that the GPO must have lost a few mailbags in the Atlantic. In the end, I had to accept that my tartan letters, had failed to tickle the fancy of whoever received them. I would have to put the second stage of my campaign into motion – my trip to America.

My plan was to convince the big department stores that they should stock a wide range of tartan goods. I would be acting as a kind of middle-man between the American shops and the Scottish manufacturers. To prepare America for my arrival, I wrote to several famous New York stores, explaining my terms and promising more details when I got there. Replies came back. They were hardly enthusiastic, but there were a couple of requests to 'drop in'. That was enough for me; I booked my passage.

I sailed from Liverpool on the *Britannic*. It was like living in a luxury hotel with nothing to do but eat, drink and play games, so it was with relief that I heard we were nearing our destination. I went on deck to view the famous New York skyline. I thought of all the immigrants, including my own relatives, who'd sailed into that harbour, in search of a new life and freedom from tyranny and persecution. I could imagine their hopes, and their misgivings.

I looked up at the Statue of Liberty, and for a brief moment I imagined that gracious lady wearing a kilt.

I went straight to Macy's and introduced myself. Nobody seemed to have heard of me. They directed me from one department to another, so that each time I had to explain myself afresh. The lingerie lady sent me to the carpet department which, in turn, sent me to gents' outfitting. My letter had obviously been lost or thrown away; possibly no one had really expected me to come all the way from Scotland to tell them about tartan goods.

I eventually found someone prepared to give me a hearing. I put everything I could into my sales talk. All the expertise I'd inherited from my father and all my marketing experience came into play as I painted a picture of American Scots pining for their homeland and desperate to spend their dollars on anything which suggested an ancestry. I wound up by offering a consignment of heraldic shields at a 'very special' price.

The man had listened quietly but the moment I finished he exploded into laughter. When he finally stopped, he came up with a good reason for not buying my shields. It was a somewhat familiar reason.

'Brother,' he drawled, 'if there are, as you say, one hundred and twenty tartans, how many shields do you expect me to order?' He produced the argument that hundreds of MacGregors, demanding shields, might march on the store and all that would be in stock would be Campbell, MacDonald or Stewart. The staff would be under siege, he claimed.

I assured him that this represented no real difficulty. Were there a mass demand for MacGregor, or any other shield, I would send the goods direct from Scotland to the customer; I was naturally, thinking of the benefits for my own proposed

109

airmail business. He saw through me immediately; well, his name *was* Joe Levy. 'Oh yeah?' he observed drily. 'That means that you get all the profits and Macy's gets left standing, with nothing. Brother you're *not* on!'

He refused to buy but I think he admired my determination to sell. 'Just wait till I get home and tell the kids this,' he said, smiling in anticipation of their enjoying the hilarious story of my visit. 'I've seen some strange things in this store but this is the first time anybody tried to sell me Scottish ancestry.' I was glad he was amused but my situation was beginning to look hopeless. I think he must have noticed the signs of depression on my face for he took me by surprise by inviting me home for dinner. I accepted gladly, grateful for a gesture of friendship, and a meal. Joe and his wife Rachel filled me to bursting point as I did my best to tell them about Scotland over the combined bawling of their five kids. Apart from the luxuriousness of the house, I might have been back in The Happy Land. I left with my head splitting but was greatly impressed by my first experience of American hospitality.

The next day I had to get back to the grind of selling. A few years earlier, I'd met a successful businessman called Harry Gold. He'd enthused to me about his commercial empire in America and insisted that if ever I crossed the Atlantic I should look him up. He was a textile agent and had large offices in New York. A telephone call was rewarded with a delighted invitation. I soon saw that he hadn't exaggerated the scale of his business. There was an abundance of secretaries, and one of them escorted me to the great man's personal suite of offices. I was ushered in to where he sat, looking exactly like a successful executive in a cartoon drawing. He was enthroned behind a vast desk and most of his large mouth was plugged with a formidable cigar. 'Be Jesus,' he welcomed me. 'If it ain't my old limey friend from Scatland.'

I thought we might get down to talking business but within two minutes he'd produced a pack of cards and was suggesting a game of gin rummy. I obviously didn't want to upset him, so I resigned myself to a game or two. He was clearly an enthusiastic player and thought it would be a laugh to fleece me. Of course, he didn't realise that his old limey friend had spent years watching and playing gin rummy back in St Leonard's Hill, and was no amateur. Money was produced and I won several games. Irritatedly, he doubled the stakes but I still continued to take his money. Harry Gold was a bad loser. 'You're as lucky as a bloody Jew,' he growled resentfully. I realised that if I allowed my luck to continue there would be precious little chance of winning any business from Harry so I deliberately made a few mistakes and, as the dollars began to trickle back across to his side of the desk, he mellowed and his smile began to reappear. When we were about even again, I tactfully suggested that we stop. He seemed to find this acceptable and I assumed that, finally, it was time to talk business.

'So,' he said, putting his cards away. I found myself wondering if every visitor to the office had to engage in a prolonged bout of gin rummy. 'What are you doing tonight, friend?' he asked.

What Harry had in mind was a hedonistic night on the town with a couple of 'broads'. I could sense that tartan scrolls were pretty low on his list of priorities so, as they say, I made my excuses and left.

Having failed to make a financial killing in New York, I decided to head to Chicago where my two uncles were living. They were leading quite different lives from one another, but I found it impossible to relate to either of them. One was a wealthy estate agent; the other dealt in scrap iron and, to my amazement, used a horse and cart. Both men had, however, a kind of brashness which I found off-putting. It contrasted with the warmth of my family in Scotland. Meeting the Chicago brothers made me grateful that my proposed emigration to the States in 1939 had been cancelled. I don't think I would have fitted in.

The estate agent gave me a half-hearted invitation to coffee at his club. It was not a successful social occasion, and I came away with the impression that my uncle was a mean man, in every sense. America had made him hard and unapproachable. The scrap dealer was more jovial, but I still felt distanced from him. There was no way I was going to nestle into the bosom of my Chicago family. I found trying to make business contacts in Chicago even tougher than in New York. I felt isolated and spent much time writing long letters home.

It was with relief that I caught a plane for the Pacific. My next destination was Vancouver, where there was no shortage of people with Scottish ancestors. For the first time since I'd sailed from Liverpool, I was in business. Stores were keen to give me orders for my bone china, rainwear, tartan socks and even my infamous scrolls. While there, I was fortunate to meet a buyer from Macy's store in Los Angeles. He said that my socks and rainwear would be too heavy for the Californian climate, but he reckoned my bone china would sell well there. That was enough for me. I settled up my business in Vancouver and was soon winging my way to Los Angeles. I breezed confidently into Macy's, only to be told that the buyer had just gone away for a few weeks. However, his assistant thought it would be worth while to wait and see him when he returned. Still flushed with my Canadian success, I decided to explore Los Angeles. Having grown up in the age of the cinema, I was excited by the idea of being so close to Hollywood.

I found myself wondering how my favourite Hollywood stars would look in kilts, or draped in tartan travelling-rugs. All that wealth around me! What a potential market! Of course I hadn't a clue how to make contact with the film world, so I phoned up a local newspaper, the *Los Angeles Examiner*. The hardbitten editor stripped me of my illusions: 'Gee buddy', he exploded down the line, 'I'm not a tourist guide and this is no introduction bureau for wandering limey troubadours'! So there I was, in one of the most exciting cities in the world, sitting alone in a hotel room.

CHAPTER NINETEEN

Escape

I was becoming increasingly confused. I found America a lonely place, and even thought nostalgically about Manchester. Yet I knew if I were there I'd want to be somewhere else. Was all this restlessness just a desire to escape from my responsibilities or was it a genuine search to find something to bring meaning to my existence? I didn't know. I would dearly have loved to have someone to discuss it with, but I was alone in a hotel in an impersonal city. Edinburgh seemed remote, and I'd allowed my relationship with my parents to dwindle. But, I told myself, attempting to be positive, I was in Los Angeles and I still had business to do. It was the opportunity of a lifetime.

I phoned Macy's and was relieved to hear that the buyer had returned from his travels. A meeting was arranged and my spirits rose when he quickly gave me a large order for bone china. There was a certain irony that, having gone to sell Scotland and Scottish ancestry, I was being successful with English china. I made a transatlantic call to my supplier in Stafford, and worked out what I thought was an excellent deal. However, after weeks of convolutions, I ended up losing money while a swindler called Sam became extremely rich. I ended my stay in America with a depressing outing to the famous Roseland Dance Hall in New York. And that ended my campaign to improve Britain's exports. In the process I'd become older and wiser, but I certainly wasn't any wealthier or happier.

I had to make a living somehow and could think of no other way but through photography. The North of England held little attraction for me any more, so I wound up the business in Manchester and attempted to re-establish myself in Edinburgh where I'd retained a studio. I didn't want just to repeat what I'd been doing before, so I racked my brain in an attempt to find something that was, at least, slightly different. As great numbers of babies had been born since the war, I decided that I should specialise in child photography. It made sense to search for business in the suburbs. At that time a lot of Edinburgh consisted of run-down slums. The high-rise estates now found on the city's fringes had yet to appear. So it was to the comfortably-off suburbs that I went in search of subjects.

My idea proved a success. Soon I was able to employ canvassers to go round the doors and arrange appointments for me. The photographs were done in the homes and so, of course, saved the families the inconvenience of a trip to the city centre. I provided proofs free of charge and invariably got a good order. So successful was the child photography that I had to employ another three photographers, as well as all the canvassers. Soon my business spread to Glasgow, Newcastle, Manchester and even London. The profits were considerable and my firm came to be regarded as specialists in photographing children.

I suppose if I were a sensible, stable kind of a person, I would have sat back and told myself that this was 'it'. I had a thriving business; all I had to do was maintain it and make sensible provision for my eventual retirement. But I was back in a situation where most of my day was devoted to making money. I'd learned, with Joan's help, that such a life was not enough; it was empty and unfulfilling. Fretting about wages and overheads didn't make me a happy man. The old ennui had returned. I was restless, yet nevertheless ploughed on with the business for some years.

I'd already dabbled in psychoanalysis and dance therapy and still had a ready interest in anything which might add an extra dimension to my life and help me to understand myself better. So when, in the late 1950s, some friends told me about a mysterious guru who was operating in the unlikely-sounding setting of Kingston-upon-Thames, my interest was immediately aroused. Could this guru be my salvation? I was ready to try.

His name was John Bennett and he taught at an institute of philosophy, science and religion. His system was based on the philosophy of G. I. Gurdjieff, the influential thinker who spent some twenty years in the remotest regions of Central Asia, from Constantinople to the Gobi Desert, learning and absorbing ancient knowledge and religions. A stay at the Institute involved Buddhism, meditation and sacred dance. I had to investigate.

I drastically reduced the scale of my business and left only the Edinburgh studio open, in the hands of a manageress. Then I packed my bags and headed south to a large mansion house called Coombe Springs.

CHAPTER TWENTY

Sanctuary

At Coombe Springs I found a regime which was to alter my whole attitude to life. The centre became my new home. When I arrived, about sixty volunteers were busy in the spacious grounds, building a temple for meditation; I was immediately invited to join in. Having no building skills, I soon found myself in the role of a rather senior tea-boy. As well as my chores, I had also to attend the talks and religious gatherings.

I found the other people somewhat solemn. Most seemed to regard the place as a retreat and were preparing themselves before returning to face the world outside. At first, I adopted an attitude of cheerfulness and was generally greeted with a reaction of faintly amused tolerance. Most of the men, perhaps to help themselves appear unworldly and intellectual, had grown beards. Thinking it best to join the club, I began to sprout my own bushy fungus. At least I now *looked* like one of the lads.

If we had any problems we were encouraged to talk to the advisers. They were people who'd been at the Institute for years and were considered well-equipped to give support in times of stress or unhappiness. The advisers were necessary as there were quite a few neurotic inmates who were almost constantly having crises. The Institute inevitably attracted such people. Not long after I arrived, a woman ran out of the gates and down a busy street in her nightdress. The police had grown used to such behaviour and if ever anyone was found doing anything unusual around the town, a phone call would come through immediately to Coombe Springs from the police station.

My activities were of no interest to the police but, after some time at the Institute, I was still feeling unsettled. I knew my problem was sex and made up my mind to seek the help of Arthur, one of the advisers. More and more women had been arriving at the Institute and I knew that my meditations were more concerned with the contours of their bodies than with any form of spiritual uplift. I felt like a fake. I was supposed to be improving myself and developing inner discipline. All I felt was lust.

'When do these thoughts occur the most?' asked Arthur.

'About twenty hours a day,' I had to admit. Arthur recommended that I work harder. So, instead of the light chores I'd been engaged in, I took to trundling wheelbarrows laden with stones. My limbs ached, but it didn't work; my fantasies refused to go away. All that happened was that the erotic activities in my imagination took place at a much increased rate.

As if on cue, a new resident arrived at Coombe Springs. She was an American opera singer, complete with hair as bright as carrots and a bosom expansive enough to contain the biggest of voices. She'd recently suffered a shattering experience and was suffering from mental and physical exhaustion. Most of the residents loved, and enjoyed, peace and quiet for their meditation. However, Lucia felt the need to practise her vocal talents at all hours. Ear-splitting arias would suddenly echo down the hallways. Arthur, my adviser, decided that two problems might be solved at once if he could team me up with Lucia. I would have an object for my desires, and my attentions might distract her from launching herself into *La traviata* or belting out *La bohème*. Unfortunately, Arthur's theory didn't work. Lucia was obsessed by her work and my overtures failed to impress her. Every time I attempted to lull her into a romantic frame of mind, she'd think of some aria relevant to the situation, and let rip. I decided to bring the curtain down on that particular episode of my life.

After several more weeks, I began to realise I'd made a mistake: I'd thrown myself from a life of money-making work into the contemplative and co-operative environment of the Institute. I'd gone from one extreme to another. What I needed was a balance. My solution was to begin work again, one day a week, as a child photographer. I felt guilty about this, so didn't tell anyone. I felt it was somehow living a lie and being a traitor to the aims of the Institute. Was it just a grasping desire for extra cash? I didn't think so. I needed the external stimulus.

So I advertised in the local press and got a woman with a car to do my canvassing. Then I borrowed her car, loaded up my equipment and slid out for a day's work. I sent the films to my Edinburgh studio for processing and the results were posted direct to the customers. It worked well, so I engaged a second woman and went out photographing two days a week. More and more postal inquiries arrived for me at the Institute and this caused a few puzzled glances to be exchanged. I was, after all, supposed to be 'in retreat' and yet was getting more mail than even the Institute secretary.

My work was again a success but I still had to deal with my guilt. My solution was to work even harder while I was at the Institute. I volunteered to be the breakfast cook every morning and this kept me engaged from seven until ten o'clock. One morning, to give myself relief from the routine, I drew comic faces on the boiled eggs. This proved to be quite an interesting social experiment: some residents appreciated my little joke but others were so involved with themselves and their inner development that they ate their breakfasts without even noticing that their eggs were grinning up at them.

A place like Coombe Springs can give people the chance to explore any artistic or creative talents they may have. My egg-heads were hardly art but I had my photography and I like to regard it as more than just a trade; I had, for a long time, felt that I could and ought to try to create something. But I didn't borrow some oil paints and go out into the garden to paint a view. It is typical of me that I had to approach the subject by means of a joke. Perhaps I was frightened of exposing my true self to the critical gaze of others. Also, I got a little fed up with the eternal seriousness of some of the people connected with Coombe Springs. I wanted, if possible, to raise a smile or two, especially on an occasion when the place was busy with visitors. So, in the grounds, I mounted my very own exhibition of abstract art. For one exhibit I grabbed a large sheet of paper, stuck some grass across the bottom of it with glue, then rubbed my bare feet in the dust and trampled over the paper. I completed the effect by adding an elastoplast to the imprint left by one of my big toes. Another of my masterworks consisted of a sheet of card to which I'd stuck a tin can, orange peel and cigarette ends. A third work developed the theme I'd first used with the boiled eggs: I employed wool and a needle to sew strange faces onto big sheets of paper. As I couldn't think of suitable titles for my works, I called the exhibition *Art Without Names*.

I stood in the grounds with my face frozen into an expression of grim seriousness. I did my utmost to look like an artist who wanted, at all costs, to be taken seriously. Some of the residents and visitors immediately realised that I couldn't possibly be serious and enjoyed the joke. Others were less perceptive. One intense man was heard to mutter, 'Most interesting,' but the image which has remained with me most clearly is of a tweed-suited woman with heavy-framed spectacles. She peered at my works then turned to her companion and made the comment, 'An extraordinary sense of the tactile.'

We eventually completed our temple of meditation in the garden. It was octagonal, and a true place of peace. Inside its walls I managed to achieve some kind of contentment, however temporary. The sunlight filtered through the leaves of the trees and entered the building, providing a warm glow. At times the light played strange tricks and made people seem to have haloes. Often, the only sound was bird-song. It was in that temple that I came fully to appreciate the benefits to be derived from meditation. I wasn't inspired enough to abandon all my worldly goods and ambitions, but I did become convinced of the importance of retaining a balance between the material and spiritual aspects of life. A result of all this was that I reduced my photography activities from two days a week back to one.

At one point, I managed to interweave the spiritual with the material by photographing a visiting Indonesian guru, selling the pictures to visitors, then donating the proceeds to the Institute. Around the same time, however, I became involved with another religious leader – a cardinal of the Roman Catholic Church.

This particularly ridiculous episode began when one of my customers asked if a painting of her daughter could be done from one of the photographs I'd taken. I knew that a Mr Goldberg had a firm which did this in the East End of London, so I approached him about the portrait. Being a shrewd man, he realised that all my business in the stockbroker belt could help him. We came to an arrangement that if I sent him business, I would be paid an appropriate commission. All I had to do was suggest the idea of a painted portrait to the parents then, if successful, send the photograph with details of the colouring to Goldberg, and his art workers would do the rest. So there I was again, making more money. It seemed as though I just couldn't help it.

I didn't want to use Coombe Springs as my trading address so I rented a mailing address in Old Bond Street, London. I engaged a publicity firm to advertise my services and soon a thousand circulars, describing me as a camera artist, were on their way to actors, businessmen, trade-union leaders and all manner of VIPs. The message was simple: they could be immortalised in oils without having to waste time sitting for an artist. Business began almost immediately when I received an order from the secretary of a big trade union, asking for portraits of two former secretaries. Everything went smoothly and I made around a hundred per cent profit on each one. Eagerly, I awaited further orders.

A call came from a famous cathedral in London. Would I photograph the cardinal, then do his portrait in oils? Certainly! I packed my equipment and the paints I used to match up the colours and made straight for the cathedral. I was greatly impressed by the importance of my mission.

An attendant ushered me into a large room already hung with

portraits. 'Of course,' he said, 'you'll know who all these are'. He waved his hand sweepingly at a row of the pictures.

'Oh, of course,' I murmured, painfully aware that they all meant absolutely nothing to me. From his subsequent conversation I gathered that the mysterious gents were all Roman Catholic kings of European countries. I couldn't help feeling like a hopelessly ignorant imposter, surrounded as I was by that powerful atmosphere of religion, history and wealth.

Eventually the cardinal had completed his preparations and I was allowed to gaze upon his person. He looked splendid and had obviously donned all his most impressive robes and paraphernalia. He wasn't going to be outdone by a lot of painted kings. I was so awestruck that I found myself approaching him on tip-toe. I could tell immediately that I had before me the perfect subject for a very striking portrait. Nervously I drew up a chair and used my paints to record the colours of his skin, hair and clothing. As I worked I was aware of his eyes on me. Seeing me with my paints, he had assumed I was the artist. He didn't know that I was sub-contracting the painting work and I sat there uncomfortably, feeling that he was trying to assess my capabilities from my amateurish daubings.

With considerably more confidence I took the required photographs and escaped with relief from the solemn room. When the photographs were printed I delivered them to Goldberg's office. 'How big is this picture to be?' he asked, not unreasonably.

I'd never thought of that. But I remembered the portraits of the Catholic kings and replied, 'Oh, about five feet by four feet or so, I should think.' A big picture.

On the way back to Coombe Springs I speculated about how much I could charge for the finished picture. I ought to have discussed the price at the cathedral but in the hallowed precincts it had seemed a somewhat sordid subject to raise. The impression I'd gained, however, was that there was no shortage of funds. I reckoned I could count on a considerable profit for my efforts.

In due course, the portrait was completed and I felt proud as I transported its considerable bulk to the cathedral. The attendant helped me to set the picture up on a chair. The cardinal strode in, went straight to the picture and scrutinised it carefully. His brows furrowed. He whispered a few words to the attendant then left. Just a few alterations, I was told. A little touch here, a slight change there. Of course, I had to haul the cumbersome thing back to Goldberg's.

In time, I arrived back at the cathedral with the touched-up version. More objections were raised. Soon I was making regular trips back and forward across London, but it was no use. After five tries, the truth began to come out. Really, the cardinal didn't like the portrait very much and, believing that I was the artist, didn't want to hurt my feelings. Hugely disappointed, I shuffled out of the cathedral for the last time, weighed down by depression, and the cardinal's portrait.

I hurried back to Goldberg's to inform him that his work had been judged unacceptable. He wasn't interested. I'd ordered it and he'd had it painted, exactly to my specifications. As far as he was concerned, that was the end of the matter. I had to pay him for the picture, and that was the end of our little business agreement.

The money I lost on the deal was about the same as I'd made from the trade-union secretaries' portraits so I was, more or less, back where I started. Except that now I was the owner of an almost life-size portrait of a Roman Catholic cardinal. This was an asset I could do without.

I knew of no one who'd buy it; I knew of no one who'd accept it as a gift. In the evening, when the trains were quieter, I carried my red-robed associate back to Coombe Springs. Some residents thought the picture was all my own work. Why else would I be carrying such a thing around with me? Others decided that I was cracking up or had had a serious bout of religious fervour. I found it impossible to give them the true story, so just left them all guessing.

Back in my room, I felt so fed up with the whole time-wasting episode that I stuck the portrait under my bed. All through the night I felt disturbed and slept badly. I wondered if I were suffering from a form of divine retribution; after all, I'd let the cardinal believe that I was the painter. I'd been less than honest. In the morning I still felt unsettled so, amid the puzzled stares of the other residents, I carried the portrait out to a disused Nissen hut in the grounds. Soon, in splendid isolation, the portrait was hanging inside the hut. Any people passing the window on a bright day would probably have been amazed to see the dignified figure of the cardinal staring out at them from his dilapidated palace of corrugated iron.

I stayed at Coombe Springs for two years. It was recommended that people stay for only three months, in order that they didn't become too divorced from the outside world. I knew my departure was overdue. But I'd done something important. Apart from my occasional sorties back into the world of work, I'd had a chance to stand back and assess my life. My values, I was sure, had been altered for the better. It was as though I'd had a holiday away from my life and I now felt calm enough to go back and face it again. I packed my bags and left.

CHAPTER TWENTY-ONE

My Homecoming

After leaving Coombe Springs in 1962, I spent a brief and unrewarding period in Liverpool. Soon, I was back in Edinburgh where I felt there was room to breathe. Once again I fell back on photography to keep body and soul together and, once again the business began to expand. I found it difficult, however, to take the same interest as I'd done before. I therefore delegated a lot of the work I should have kept an eye on. The result was that the finances went adrift and I ended up close to bankruptcy. I just managed to avoid this stigma by selling my assets and being granted two years to repay my creditors. I needed to find a source of income, quickly.

My parents were still in Edinburgh and by then were living in Dalkeith Road. They shared the house with Sydney, my youngest brother, and soon made room for me, their prodigal son. Mother and Sydney welcomed me back with open arms but Father couldn't resist some barbed comments. He described me as the rich man who lost all his gelt and had to come crawling back. On my previous visits I'd chosen not to partake of home comforts and had stayed in good hotels. Father didn't let me forget that. He continued to be very critical but, after a while, I grew immune to his comments. As an experienced adult I could no longer regard him as an opponent. I could understand his resentment. Also, I could see the many strengths in this man who'd struggled against odds to give his family a home. Looking back, I now realise how generous my parents were to take me back after all the things I'd done: I'd played the big shot, adopted some very odd ideas, then lost all my money; and worst of all, I'd failed to marry a nice Jewish girl. In their own different ways, they managed to forgive me. I stayed with them for about two years.

For some time I'd been calling myself Howard Denton rather than Hyman Zoltie. I'd wanted a name which didn't immediately suggest that I was a foreigner, an outsider. I'd expected that my rejection of the family name might upset my parents but I needn't have worried. I discovered that Father was in the drapery trade and, for business purposes, was calling himself Mr Morris. He never took the trouble to become naturalised as he had an inbuilt distrust of all officialdom. His dislike of paperwork got him into muddles over income tax; he never bothered with records or accounts. Nevertheless, he continued to trade successfully until he was over seventy.

Karl had married during my long absence and eventually took over Father's business as the old man grew less able. Reuben's marriage to his Spanish wife ended in divorce. His second wife was Jewish and he was duly welcomed back into the fold. He was devoted to our parents and, whenever possible, showered them with gifts or paid for them to go on holiday. Motty had also taken a Jewish wife but his marriage was the result of professional matchmaking. It was known that he enjoyed having money, so he was introduced to, and subsequently married, a Glasgow woman with a considerable dowry. Her parents set them up in comfort in Glasgow, but stress soon resulted from Motty's love of gambling; he also had an eye for other women. In his business deals he was sometimes less than honest and made Father extremely angry. So sour did their relationship become that they almost ended up in court in an argument over a three-piece suite. As usual, it was Motty who was in the wrong.

I'd been dragged away from school at the age of fourteen and put straight into a tailor's workshop. I've always felt this was a waste. After I'd left home, some of Father's friends tried to make him see that a good education was something worthwhile; it could, in fact, be an investment. They succeeded in convincing him that my younger brothers Jack and Sydney should be allowed to stay on at school. Both brothers graduated from university.

Lena married a solicitor and went to live near Aberdeen.

Whenever they visited Edinburgh, Father took every opportunity to try to extract free legal advice from his son-in-law. Anna, always volatile and indomitable, went through a variety of jobs before emigrating to America with her second husband. Ella was always quiet and went to work in an office. She also kept quiet about the fact that when she got married she was already pregnant. Dark-skinned Betty continued to show an interest in coloured boys: she disappeared to London and married a West Indian postman. So the crumbs of the family cake were well scattered, with only Sydney and me living at home with our parents.

Despite a degree in Mining Engineering, Sydney took no interest in the possibilities open to him in the oil industry, particularly in the Middle East. He chose to follow Father's footsteps and had a string of successful dress shops in Edinburgh. Meanwhile, I was just drifting aimlessly and Mother was obviously worried about me.

'Hoy, Hymie, what am I going to do with you?' she would sigh. 'Why don't you start a leetle business like Sydney here in Edinburgh and maybe settle down with a nice Jewish girl?' I remember telling her categorically that I had absolutely no money to start any kind of business. She took me by surprise. 'Here,' she said, and pressed £50 into my hand. 'But don't tell your father. Maybe this will help you to start something. I don't know what.' I had great difficulty holding back my tears. Her gesture made me aware of how much she loved me and how she still could have faith in me after all the mistakes I'd made. Her action jolted me into activity. I wanted to show her I was worthy of her belief in me.

I didn't use the £50 to start a business. I couldn't. It may seem sentimental but I put the money in an envelope and wrote 'From Mum' on the outside. I put it in a safe deposit, intending never to spend it. It was so much more than £50 to me; it was an inspiration.

I began once more to rack my brain and walk the streets looking for ideas. At that time there was a large building in the historic Royal Mile which was due for demolition. I made inquiries and discovered that Edinburgh Corporation was offering to lease the accommodation on a monthly basis. I took on a shop with extra rooms upstairs. It seemed a mad gamble. I'd no idea what to do with the shop and I could face eviction at any time.

Sydney lent me the money for the first month's rent and soon I was installed in my near-derelict premises. I was determined to do something new. I wanted nothing connected with photography or any of my previous ventures. At the time, the record industry was showing signs of expanding but only in London were there large shops devoted wholly to selling records. In the rest of Britain, people tended to buy from stores such as Boots or from local radio and electrical goods shops. The 33 and 45 rpm discs had largely replaced the old brittle 78s, but there were many music fans, particularly the not-so-young ones, who had large collections of 78s and played them regularly. Anyone who bought a record player at the time found that it came with facilities for playing different speeds of disc. It was relatively easy to buy the latest 45 rpm hit records but there was nowhere, apart from the occasional junk shop, where an enthusiast could go and browse through 78s. I decided to fill that gap and specialise in Scottish dance music. That seemed a sensible move in the most historic street of Scotland's capital city.

Sydney helped me to prepare the shop and, with his car, we collected box upon box of second-hand 78s. I advertised in the press and after days of sorting, cleaning and indexing I was ready for the customers. There was a queue of bargain hunters at the door on my opening day and, over the next few weeks, business built steadily. It seemed as if I'd successfully filled a gap in the market.

After a while, however, my racks began to empty. I'd exhausted all the sources of old 78s that I could think of and, of course, there was no recognised supplier. My solution was to become a record exchange. I asked customers to bring in their old records and exchange them for new ones. That, however, was easier said than done. I was not an officially recognised record retailer and, at that time, was not permitted to buy new records from the wholesalers. I was forced to go to other shops and pay retail prices for new LPs by Sinatra, Presley and Buddy Holly. I then put these on display, giving the shop, I thought, a more up-market appearance. Inevitably, some customers were puzzled by the fact that I wouldn't sell these new records but could only part with them on an exchange basis.

I've always seen myself as a reasonably good businessman but Sydney was of the opinion that I could be too soft-centred for my own good. He wanted to see me being successful and said I'd have to be more ruthless when it came to doing exchanges with my customers. I followed his advice but didn't like it. I felt dishonest.

One morning a man came in with about forty records wrapped in newspaper. There was nothing wrong with them but I put on a poker-face and solemnly sorted my way through them. 'A bit worn,' I said. 'And not much demand for this sort of thing.' He looked disappointed. 'I'm afraid,' I continued, 'I can't offer you more than half a dozen in exchange for these.'

'You mean only six?' he asked in surprise.

I nodded. He was very unhappy about the offer but was unwilling to cart the forty heavy records all the way home and so, grudgingly, accepted. I felt like a rogue.

Then Sydney made another suggestion. 'Why don't you deal in second-hand pop records? The kids get fed up with their records after a few weeks, when they're no longer in the hit parade.' I advertised accordingly and soon my first batch of pop arrived. A lad came into the shop and dumped a pile of fairly recent hit singles on the counter. He had his eye on the brand new Shadows LP on display behind me. I acted hard again.

'Oh, I'm afraid you don't have enough records for that one,' I said firmly. An hour later, he arrived back with more of his old singles and went off clutching his Shadows LP. I had my first stock of pop singles and exchanged them as successfully as I'd done with the Scottish 78s.

Some of my clients were in desperate need of hard cash and I'm afraid I offered ridiculously low sums for their bundles of records. They usually accepted my offers, however, as they had no other way to get hold of some ready money.

One day I had difficulty maintaining my typical lack of expression when a young man arrived with forty brand new LPs. Compared with old 78s, the LPs were like gold to me. I took a chance and offered him £20, which was about one third of what the records would cost retail. He jumped at my offer and disappeared. Of course, the minute he'd gone I began to worry in case they were stolen. I remembered how Father had only just escaped jail when he'd sold stolen cigarettes in his Grassmarket shop. Nervously, I dirtied the glossy new covers to make them look like good second-hand records but I needn't have bothered as no suspicious policemen arrived at the shop.

Apart from hearing the occasional band on the BBC Light Programme, I'd known very little about music before the Record Exchange. I found my knowledge increasing daily. I played records all day, as I found that doing so definitely increased business. I knew absolutely nothing about classical music and was wary when someone arrived with LPs of music by Beethoven and Mozart. I gave him my usual disparaging routine but accepted the records. To my amazement, they were snapped up immediately and so, from then on, I happily added classical discs to my stock. I gave myself something of a musical education by listening to them in the evenings, after the shop was closed. I was thoroughly enjoying my little corner of the record business, though I still felt ill at ease when offering people what I myself thought were poor prices or exchange deals. But then, they didn't have to accept my offers; the choice was theirs.

By accident, I thought of a way to salve my conscience. A pensioner came in one day and began to browse through the old 78s. He was unshaven and wore an old black suit and worn-out sandals. His cloth cap was pulled down over his eyes. I watched him out of interest as it was unusual for me to get elderly customers.

I could see his hands shaking as he sorted his way awkwardly through the old Regal Zonophones and Brunswicks. After an age, he approached the counter with a well-worn copy of Jimmy Shand reels. I didn't have the heart to charge him anything, so muttered something about not being able to get rid of that particular record. The delight that appeared in his eyes gave me an idea. I had hundreds of old records taking up room. Some were so ancient that only Thomas Edison would have known what to do with them. I was sure they'd never sell, but suspected that they'd be enjoyed by old folk who would remember them from their youth. I offered them to old people's homes and they were gratefully accepted, making me feel, for a while, like the Good Samaritan.

Around that time, a friend arrived with an interesting piece of news. A factory which made records had been damaged by fire in London. The records were to be sold off cheaply by auction. I took a chance and flew down the following day. There were thousands of LPs and singles, many with only their sleeves damaged. They couldn't be sold in normal record shops but they were perfect for my Record Exchange. The factory was like an Aladdin's cave to me. I spent a whole day choosing what I knew would sell in Edinburgh and bought them for less than half the wholesale price. I passed them on to the public at bargain prices but still made a profit.

There were so many records at the London factory that I seemed to have discovered a limitless supply of cheap commercial stock. I was able to open another exchange in central Glasgow. Business thrived there, too, and I found myself dealing less in the old cracked 78s. Feeling like a tycoon, I flew regularly to London and selected more batches of cheap records. Sometimes I even travelled first class and bought myself cigars.

In summer, Edinburgh becomes packed to bursting point with visitors who come from all over the world for the annual Festival. I knew it would make sense if I could get myself a shop in busy Princes Street, opposite the castle and Princes Street Gardens.

I was surely on a winning streak as, just at the right time, I was able to take over a big shop at the corner of Princes Street and Frederick Street. It is now quite common for shops to deafen passers-by with raucous music, but I think I may have been the first shopkeeper to flood Princes Street with melody. It was Scottish country dance music which skirled its lively way among the holidaymakers and culture seekers. The sound was relayed through a grille and people would wonder where on earth the fiddler and accordionist were. Puzzled pedestrians would cross to Princes Street Gardens to see if there was a concert on at the Ross bandstand. Eventually the entertainment would be traced to my shop and inevitably I would draw in customers. The shop specialised in Scottish music and there was, at the time, one record which visitors couldn't hear often enough – *A Scottish Soldier* by Andy Stewart. I must admit that I grew sick of the song but I had to stock it, to keep the customers satisfied. Luckily for me, the factory in London had a virtual regiment of Scottish Soldiers; I convinced the boss there that they would never sell in London and so got the lot at a price which allowed me to make four hundred per cent profit.

My prices, naturally, were undercutting those of all the other Edinburgh stores. And they didn't like it. I was still not recognised as an official record retailer and still couldn't get my stocks from the wholesalers but, with my London supplies of cheap records, I'd successfully solved all my problems. An investigator arrived one day to find out where I was getting my bargain records from. I told him quite readily. It was all quite legitimate and there was little my competitors could do about it. I did, however, receive a solicitor's letter about the noise outside my shop. All I did was disconnect the loudspeaker from the grille and turn up the volume of the record player inside the shop.

To attract more visitors, I hired a character called Rory McPherson. All he had to do was stand outside the shop in full Highland dress. He was over six feet tall and, in his kilt, bonnet and tartan plaid, impossible to miss. Visitors from abroad would stop to stare at him, hear the music then come inside to part with their dollars, marks or francs. I sold them a memory of Scotland.

Unfortunately, Rory found it necessary to complete his image of the perfect Scot by fuelling himself with whisky. There were times when I feared his breath might ignite and he would explode in a tartan fireball. Also, with so much time on his hands, he felt he could woo the lassies. In short, he began to make a nuisance of himself with the female staff and, after a few warnings, I had to send him on his tartan way.

The holiday season ended and so, eventually, did my supply of cheap records. I closed the Princes Street shop, having made enemies of all the retailers nearby. Next, I shut the Glasgow Record Exchange. I'd grown tired of the repeated journeys back and forward. It was time to think of a new venture.

CHAPTER TWENTY-TWO

Entering the World of Food and losing my dentures in Spain

My Edinburgh Record Exchange in the Royal Mile was still ticking over but I was on the scent of a fresh challenge. Nearby, there were several empty premises. I could imagine them all as successful businesses run by yours truly. Being in the city centre and on the tourist trail, I felt that the right kind of restaurant, one that was fast and efficient, was bound to be a success. I'd always loved food but it had never occurred to me that I could make a living out of feeding people. I knew nothing about running a restaurant so decided to visit an old friend who did. I went to see Horace de Marco.

Horace was a successful restaurateur. I'd met him ten years earlier, through a *New Statesman* advertisement. The purpose of the advertisement had been to bring together thinkers to form a discussion group. I could hardly describe myself as a great intellectual but I've always enjoyed discussing and debating. I got on well with Horace.

He was a man of strongly-held opinions and didn't suffer fools gladly. As a result, he had few friends, but what friends he had were good ones. In his younger days he'd been a natural rebel and had been expelled from college where he was studying dentistry. As well as running his restaurant, he found time to perform classical music. He was an accomplished violinist. I was grateful that he also found time to advise me.

With his expertise and my usual enthusiasm for anything new, we soon established a restaurant which we christened The Buttery. I only had £100 at the time but Horace seemed to have unlimited access to credit facilities. We specialised in salads, soups and home baking. I can still remember the aroma of the freshly-baked bread wafting into the cold Edinburgh air.

Horace worked me hard. I did twelve hours a day for a year. Sometimes I wanted to rebel but, deep down, I was convinced his methods were right. He taught me that the public expected and had to be given the highest standards when buying meals.

At that time, he was rethinking the ideas behind *his* restaurant. Years ahead of today's fads and fancies, Horace was concerned with healthier eating and, towards that end, installed his own bakehouse in the basement of his restaurant. Then he introduced a new range of tempting salads. When I saw the queues of customers forming, I realised there could be a profitable future in healthy foods. I made up my mind to have nothing to do with canned soups, mince pies, sausage rolls and other stodge.

The Buttery, our joint effort, was as successful as Horace's own restaurant. It was a risky venture. A great deal of money had to be spent to make the premises functional as well as attractive, and Edinburgh Corporation had the right to demolish the building at any time. Still, we pressed on regardless and the gamble paid off. I enjoyed running a restaurant. I found it fulfilling to provide a service which gave pleasure to the public. In short, I was hooked. I still am today.

With The Buttery thriving, I had less interest in my nearby Record Exchange but, feeling optimistic, was inspired to use the premises for a quite different purpose. In a magazine, I'd read about a company called Vista Tours. They specialised in holidays for single people and were, in effect, a kind of introduction bureau. I remembered that such bureaux could be extremely successful, for the operators at least. It occurred to me that I could act as the Edinburgh agent for Vista Tours and therefore get a little extra income from the commission. I knew there were lots of lonely people. Despite my own busy life I still felt isolated.

After a couple of phone calls and a trip to London, I reached an agreement with the firm. I became their Scottish agent and installed a booking kiosk in the Record Exchange. I had to pay for my own advertising but was lucky to get a promotional article in the local paper. The inquiries began. No one ever actually said that he or she was looking for romance. We would discuss the travel, the accommodation, the food, the beach, but never the possibility of finding a partner. That was understood.

Vista used coaches and most of the holidays were in Italy or Spain. I had to make sure that each coach party consisted of twenty men and twenty women. Many of the customers were shy and tended to be middle-aged. I assumed that some were divorcees and others were just people who felt that life was passing them by. It is quite common for holiday companies to suggest in their advertising that a holiday is an opportunity for romance. My adverts were no different and I suspected that many clients looked forward to their Vista holidays. Some saw it as the chance of a lifetime. Others, perhaps, saw it as their last chance.

One day, a pretty woman with blonde hair arrived at the booking kiosk. She looked about twenty-two and I couldn't imagine why she'd want to go on a lonely hearts' holiday. But she did; she wished to go to Spain, so I duly booked her onto the appropriate coach. Then I had one of my ideas. I got on the phone to Vista Tours.

'It has occurred to me,' I explained, 'that if I'm selling your holidays, I really ought to know what they're like. I mean, I should get to experience one for myself.'

There was a silence at the other end.

'I was thinking, perhaps, of a short trip to Spain. Then I'd be in a better position to advise the customers.'

My idea was greeted with an obvious reluctance but, as I'd secured a healthy number of bookings, Vista decided that it was best to humour me. I promptly booked myself onto the same coach as Vicky, my young customer.

The hopeful party assembled at Victoria Station in London. Many were clearly nervous but one or two were already glancing at the opposite sex, wondering about their chances. We flew from

Gatwick, but landed at Ostend. The luxury was over. We were going all the way to southern Spain by coach. It was one of the most gruelling journeys of my life and seemed designed to destroy any possible thoughts of romance. It was an ordeal and I could understand why Vista were reluctant to let me experience what I was selling. The seats were cramped and the sun beat through the windows. We were hungry and thirsty and the coach seemed to drone on for ever across flat countryside. On top of that, being beside thirty-nine sweating strangers has never been my idea of a social event. I found their chat grating on my nerves. Some relief was provided by the guide, who was a university student on vacation. He'd already done five of these journeys and was lively company. I had to admire his powers of endurance.

The coach journey was nearly fifteen hundred miles long. Sometimes we slept as the coach hurtled through the night. At other times we were booked into small hotels with limited facilities. After several days of this, I began to lose my sense of time but eventually, crumpled and drained, we arrived at our destination, a kind of Spanish boarding-house. If we hadn't needed a holiday before we set out, we certainly needed one now. The sense of relief was almost tangible.

I still had enough strength left to have some stirrings of interest in Vicky, my real reason for undertaking the journey. I wondered what the sleeping arrangements would be. My inquiries revealed that some of my fellow travellers would be sleeping up to four in a room. Hardly a romantic situation, I thought. As an employee of Vista, however, I was blessed with a single room. I crawled into bed and passed out with exhaustion.

The supposed highlight of our stay was to be an organised tour of various bodegas where we would sample Spanish wines. That took place on our first full day there. I suspect it was included to make people forget about their coach trip.

At that time, few British people were used to drinking wine and they were unaware of the appalling after-effects that can result from over-indulgence. When the party learned that all the wine was free, they went absolutely mad. Offers of biscuits and cheese were ignored as glass after glass of red, white, sweet, dry and vinegary plonk splashed down the assembled gullets. Before long, a Blackpool-style knees-up was in full swing and the high spirits only began to abate when four or five of the party were uncontrollably sick. Fortunately, the coach driver abstained. As well as having to transport the inebriated back to the boarding-house, he also had to drag two unconscious members of the party into the coach and lay them out carefully in the aisle.

The following day I was feeling delicate. I'd not been as abandoned as some of the others but I needed to be refreshed. What better to revive me than a plunge into the surf? I approached Vicky and asked her if she fancied going for a swim. I was delighted to hear her say yes.

The beach was just like the one on the front of our brochures, except that there seemed to be a few thousand extra sunbathers. We picked our way through the yards of reddening flesh and eventually reached the sea. It felt chilly but I had to make a good impression on Vicky. With an enthusiastic whoop I plunged into the waves and swam a few strokes. It felt good. My body seemed to be tingling all over. I put my feet down on the sand and shouted to Vicky, who was hovering apprehensively at the edge. 'Come in! It's great!' At that precise moment, an enormous wave reared up and broke against my back, sending me stumbling forward. I went under but got quickly back to my feet, coughing out the salty water. When the water cleared from my eyes I could see Vicky laughing and I began to laugh myself. But I quickly shut my mouth. There was something wrong. Very wrong. Where my gleaming white teeth ought to have been, there were big gummy spaces. With rising horror I realised that my dentures had fallen out of my mouth. Desperately, I peered down into the water. All I could see was sand and my own pale feet under the water. There was a considerable undertow and I suspected my precious teeth were being steadily hauled out to the depths of the Mediterranean. As quickly as I could, I waded back out into the deeper water, staring downwards in the hope of glimpsing a tell-tale flash of white. I'm not a great swimmer so when the water reached my chest I was beginning to admit defeat. My choppers were gone. Before long, a little crab might be making a home in them.

By now, Vicky was splashing around in the shallow water. I would have to rejoin her, toothless. What hope had I of winning her affection with my sunken cheeks and my pink gums? I began to wade forlornly back to the beach and the sun-baked hordes who seemed to me to be waiting with the sole purpose of laughing at me. But wait! Aah! I stood on something hard and hurt my foot. But the pain didn't bother me. In a second I was down in the water, scrabbling about in the sand. My hand gripped something cold and hard. Yes! I rose up through the water with the speed of a dolphin. I felt triumphant. Until I looked down and saw that I was clutching an unopened can of sardines.

'What's that?' Vicky called.

'Mmm, mmm,' I hummed unhelpfully, my lips tightly sealed. I flung the sardines out to sea. Back on the beach, I began to put on my shirt. Vicky tried to chat with me but my only replies were nods and grunts.

'You're very quiet,' she commented. 'Aren't you speaking to me?'

'Yef,' I said. We returned to the boarding-house in silence. I managed to mumble that I wasn't feeling too good and wouldn't be having dinner.

Cringing with embarrassment, I crept up to my room, aware that Vicky was staring after me. I stayed in hiding until I felt it was late enough for everyone to have finished dinner. Then I slid down to the dining-room and sat down in isolation. Before long, Vicky came looking for me. She seemed actually to like me and that made the loss of my dentures doubly annoying. She watched me delicately pick my way through some bread with the crusts cut off and a slice of melon. This convinced her that I must be ill and she wanted to stay and be sympathetic. My response was to upset her by hissing that I wanted to be alone.

138

The journey back to Ostend was horrific. Not only did I have all the expected discomforts, I also had to cope with my toothlessness. Once in Edinburgh, I closed down my holiday booking kiosk. The lonely hearts of Edinburgh would have to find another way of making friends. I'd had enough. Not surprisingly, I never saw Vicky again. She must have decided I was very rude. I moved into the rooms above the Record Exchange and, like a hermit, stared out over the Royal Mile, brooding on my next move.

CHAPTER TWENTY-THREE

Beginnings and Endings

The Buttery continued to thrive but, as ever, I felt incomplete. My yearning to do something artistic began to grow again. I had a friend who taught drawing and painting and, at the time, he used to visit me in my Royal Mile rooms. Tommy was going through a low period in his life and seemed to want just to talk and talk. I thought it might take him out of himself if he were to attempt to initiate me into the world of art. He agreed and, in exchange for food, beer and a shoulder to cry on, he gave me lessons. After about six months I felt confident enough to work on my own.

I produced about twenty pictures but felt dissatisfied with just having them propped up around my rooms. I wanted to exhibit them but knew that with my amateur status no gallery would consider me. I was certain there must be hundreds of other weekend painters who felt the same as I did. I decided to do something that might help us all.

One of my upstairs rooms was long enough to be converted into a gallery, so I made up my mind to mount an exhibition of amateur art, including my own. Being situated in the busy Royal Mile could only be an advantage and there was always the chance that I might help to discover some unknown genius.

I thought I should paint a few more pictures myself, and then exhibit the best of them. What I needed was a live model so I went to the local paper to place an advertisement. I read out my requirements to the girl behind the desk. She looked at me strangely then said, 'Excuse me a minute, sir'. She disappeared through to a back room and reappeared with a stern-looking gentleman, presumably her boss.

'We can't put this sort of thing in the paper, I'm afraid,' he said, staring at me accusingly.

'What do you mean?' I asked.

'Well, you're asking for female models, aren't you?'

'Yes.'

'Well, we only accept such adverts from professional artists,' he explained. There was nothing I could do but slink out, feeling like some dirty old man.

Eventually the paper accepted an advertisement which stated that an artist was looking for subjects to paint: people or animals. Before long, my phone began to ring. Many of the callers were pet-owners who were convinced that it would do my painting career no end of good if I were to do a portrait of their dog or budgie. 'I have this marvellous alsatian, a wonderfully expressive face,' one woman told me. I hastily excused myself by saying that I already had quite a number of alsatians on my books. I had calls from mothers, each of whom had the most beautiful child or baby in the world. One man wanted to discuss body-building with me and wished to know if I took an interest in the male physique.

Some strange characters began to turn up to be interviewed when word got round that I was looking for models. Old men shuffled up from the lodging-houses in the Grassmarket. Young men with flamboyant clothes and mannerisms seemed extremely keen to do some posing for me. In the end, I found two women who were happy to act as models.

I produced more pictures of my own, then made contact with other aspiring artists. I transformed my long room into a gallery and put on the exhibition. There were no fanfares, just a decent review in the Edinburgh *Evening News*. Only a few of the paintings were sold but I had undertaken the project more for love than money, so I didn't mind. I had the pleasure of helping to promote two artists whom I remember particularly. One was the mother of a polio victim. I thought her work was excellent and she went on to sell many more of her pictures. The other was an unemployed miner from Fife. He did his paintings on hardboard and they proved popular. I was so sure of being able to sell his work that I could pay him in advance. Unfortunately, his wife died and he seemed to lose interest in life, including his painting.

I kept the gallery going for a year. It was more a hobby than anything else. I liked the atmosphere. All sorts of fascinating people trailed in and out. Beatniks, students, would-be philosophers and artists were happy to drop in for coffee and a discussion. Matters were helped by the fact that we were almost opposite the original premises of the famous Traverse Theatre and visitors would wander back and forward across the steep cobbled street. These were good times and I look back on ther with affection. However, it was soon time again to get my nose back into the world of business.

It has never been my way to work for, or even with, other people. I always felt that The Buttery had, inevitably, a fair bit of Horace de Marco's personality stamped on it and I was beginning to hanker after a restaurant that was my own. I mentioned this to Horace, wondering if he would object. After all, I would be setting up in competition. 'Mind?' he asked. 'Certainly not! I'll give you all the help you need.' And he did.

Shortly afterwards, a shop near Edinburgh University became vacant and by a happy coincidence the property was owned by one of Horace's uncles, a tough Italian businessman. He liked to rent out his properties on short leases but I persuaded him to let me have a long lease. That in itself was quite a coup and surprised Horace.

I'd had a great love of food for as long as I could remember. I have Mother to thank for that. She never failed to produce meals which were mouth-watering, even when money was short. Now The Buttery had fuelled my imagination and I became fascinated by colours, textures and aromas. I wanted to know about spices and every kind of foreign dish. Partly as a result of Horace's influence, I continued to be inspired by the idea of healthy food.

Like The Buttery, my new restaurant was self-service. This was obviously popular with people who only had an hour for lunch or were out shopping. There were plenty of establishments in Edinburgh where the better-off customer could linger over three courses with coffee and wine. I wasn't going to compete with that market. It was also a consideration that a quick turnover of customers meant faster profits.

I wanted decor which matched my idea of healthy, more natural eating. Sturdy pine tables, rough hewn stone walls and pieces of forged ironwork seemed just right, along with warm lighting. Similar decor is quite common nowadays and even perhaps something of a cliché, but in the 1960s it was a new look for a restaurant and it is a style which still proves popular. I thought hard about a name for my new baby. Finally, I settled for The Farmhouse. The name had all the right associations and had the bonus of suggesting a kind of oasis in the middle of a bustling city.

I derived great pleasure from working on the menus and decoration, but went to bed often with my head aching as a result of the seemingly endless problems with planning permission, tenders, estimates and the fire and health regulations. I was very fortunate to have Horace helping me in those early days. He was always ready to give me the benefit of his expertise and without him I'd have made many mistakes.

Horace lived his life with tireless energy. It was therefore a shock when I learned that, at the age of forty-five, he was suffering from cancer. He found it difficult to accept that his life was draining away when he had so much to live for. He was taken into the Royal Infirmary, only a few minutes from my Farmhouse. A priest arrived to comfort him but Horace sent him away. For a long time he'd felt unable to accept the Catholic faith still shared by most of his family and friends. He was a strong individualist. When I visited him in hospital, he would ask about the Farmhouse and I liked to think that he saw me, in a way, as a successor, carrying on his ideas. His death left me isolated.

Building up the restaurant kept me busy. But soon after Horace's death, I had an even worse trial to undergo. Mother, too, was discovered to have cancer and, after a stay in hospital, was sent home to die. Father was never actually told this but I'm sure he knew. Their home, which had for so many years seethed with vitality, became a place of grief. Father had to watch helplessly as Mother groaned in agony. Sometimes when I went to visit, he would be sitting alone, crying. I found this uncontrolled emotion difficult to come to terms with; all his life, Father had kept his feelings hidden from us – except for his anger. Mother was seventy-four and she and Father had been inseparable since he'd first met her in Leeds all those years before. I suspect that, in his way, he was angry because he could do nothing to help her.

A nurse came daily to give Mother a merciful dose of morphia. Mother didn't know what she was getting, or why, and used to manage to joke with the girl. We kept up a nightly vigil, knowing that there wasn't much time left. My thoughts were full of how much she'd given us all and how, inevitably, we'd taken her presence for granted, sure that she'd always be there.

All the family were together when the inevitable day came but not everyone had the strength to remain in the room for her last moments. Mother's final words have stayed with me. Her faith was as strong as ever when she died, yet she gave up her struggle with the harrowing questions: 'How do I die? What do I do?'

The Jewish faith demanded that all the male members of the family attend the synagogue twice a day for six months after her death. I found this ritual show of respect repellent and unnecessary, a piece of ostentation. I held my mother in undying regard and resented being told how to grieve for her.

Father didn't last long without his Kootky. He fell ill and was taken into hospital where he died shortly after. The doctors said it was a heart attack.

When Mother was ill, Sydney had fallen in love and quietly got married. As his wife was a Christian, the wedding was kept secret from Mother, in order not to distress her, though I'm sure that she suspected. After her death, Sydney and his wife had a baby and the last time I saw Father looking happy was when he held his grandson during the ritual of circumcision.

CHAPTER TWENTY-FOUR

Glasgow Fare

After the death of my parents I was lucky to have my busy Farmhouse Restaurant to occupy me. And so successful was the formula that I was eventually able to open more Farmhouses in the city centre, including one on Princes Street, opposite Edinburgh Castle.

When I'd had my photographic studios, and the record exchanges, I'd found the temptation to expand difficult to resist. It was the same with the Farmhouses. I was aware that on the other side of Scotland there was a bigger city which at that time had nothing to compare with my Farmhouses and their emphasis on quick, healthy meals.

I'd heard quite a bit about Glasgow's reputation for heart disease and was convinced that these grim statistics must in part be due to the Glaswegian habit of eating stodge. What more stimulating challenge therefore could I set myself than to open a Glasgow restaurant serving healthy food? Serving the food was the easy part; getting the restaurant open was another matter.

My chosen site was a basement so large that it seemed to stretch for ever. Could such a depressing expanse ever be a homely restaurant? I had my doubts. Another problem was that Glasgow was, for me, an unknown quantity. But I'd been told that the people were friendly, particularly when compared with the citizens of Edinburgh, with their lofty castle, ranks of grey Georgian houses and, dare I say it, reserved personalities. I felt optimistic about doing business with Glaswegians.

Work eventually began in the basement. And it went on, and on, until I found it impossible to remember a time when I didn't have an underground building-site with hordes of workmen. Every so often there would be an accident, a dispute or even a burglary, just to break the monotony. I got so depressed I even believed there was a plot to stop me opening my restaurant.

The strain began to wear me down. I'd recently met and married my wife Alma and I must have been hell to live with. Fortunately it was also around then that I first encountered the delights of the sauna, which helped to keep me sane. Amid the steam I would dream of the opening of my restaurant and how, single-handedly, I would convert the ailing population of Glasgow to a regime of wholesome eating. I would probably, in time, read my name in the Honours List – for services to digestive tracts.

Eventually, however, the last workman left and it was time for the opening. I was as nervous as a prima donna on a first night. Customers dribbled in. I got the impression that they would only buy if they were convinced they were getting their money's worth.

'What's that there, then?' asked a man with a huge cap. He pointed a nicotine-stained finger at a steaming container. 'What's the broon stuff?'

'Chicken and vegetable curry,' I explained.

'Ah well. Gie's some o' that, then,' he said.

I have to admit that when he was finished I wandered past casually, just to check his plate. It was scraped clean. I felt I was on my way. By noon there was a queue waiting for lunch. Then the water system sprang a leak. In a flash, water was flooding under the kitchen door and slopping around my customers' shoes. My staff dashed everywhere with mops and buckets, but it took an hour for a plumber to arrive. By mid-afternoon the flow had been stopped and the plumber said, 'Whoever installed that set-up was a *right* cowboy. My kid could do better.'

About an hour later, water again began to trickle under the kitchen door. It was the same leak, and so the same plumber returned and, with a face like fury, put right his own handiwork. Despite an electricity cut on my second day, I soldiered on and soon, built up a steady trade.

Directly above my basement restaurant there was another which had been there for twenty-five years but which suddenly went bankrupt. I was hardly surprised, as it was dull and old-fashioned. I was now in a position to grow and prosper.

So pleased was I with my bright, attractive restaurant that I used to prowl up and down like a floor-walker. I wanted to see people enjoying themselves and I was always, I must admit, ready to receive compliments. With a trained eye I checked the sizes of the portions and took to placing leaflets on the tables, explaining the aims of the restaurant.

This Farmhouse was my fifth successful restaurant. I continued to live in Edinburgh and travelled to Glasgow daily. But of course nothing ever runs perfectly. As in any business, I had staffing problems – and customer ones, too. One day, two lads came in. They looked a bit scruffy. I became suspicious when they headed straight for the toilet. I decided to keep a wary eye open but in time they emerged and joined the queue at the counter. I concluded that I was being too untrusting. They just wanted to eat, like everyone else.

But after they'd gone, a woman member of staff came to me in a panic. Someone had been in the cloakroom and taken her purse from her pocket. Eventually we traced the purse to the toilet, where it was stuffed behind the cistern. Three pounds were missing. And that was what the lads had paid for their lunch. It was difficult not to admire their nerve but I made up my mind not to ignore my hunches in future. It also occurred to me, as I paid back the three pounds, that I'd have to examine my security arrangements.

While attending to this, I never gave a thought to the street outside. Situated as I was, three minutes from a major Glasgow railway station, I'd decided that my Farmhouse Restaurant lacked the genuine earthy atmosphere of the farmyard. I'd helped to make up for this by having a welder fit two large cart-wheels to the outside wall. But one night some obviously strong and healthy characters trundled them round to the backyard and played games

147

with them, rolling them up and down until they were damaged. Another night someone took a fancy to my decorative row of gilded horseshoes. Less dramatic, but equally annoying, was the constant disappearance of my cruet sets. Even the food had a habit of vanishing before it was even prepared or cooked.

I used to keep crates of fruit just inside the back door as the atmosphere there was cool and airy. Unfortunately, I'd leave three dozen oranges and go back to find three. In such situations you tend to suspect your staff and, if you're not careful, bad feelings develop. I made up my mind to play Sherlock Holmes, but the only way I could watch unobserved was to hide behind a huge metal refuse bin in the yard.

After three days, I was surprised to see a bedraggled dog begin to sniff at a crate of cherries. Before I could yell, it raised a leg and relieved itself over the fruit. I was just about to dump the fruit in the bin when I became aware of whispering voices. I dived behind the bin again, just as two teenagers came creeping round the corner. It was the same two who'd been in the restaurant when the money went missing. I remained silent as they edged to the door, peeped inside and scooped an armful of dripping cherries into a carrier bag. I did nothing. Later, I imagined them devouring their spoils. 'Hey Tam! Don't you think these cherries have got a funny taste?'

CHAPTER TWENTY-FIVE

The Pottery

Nearly all my working life has been spent in cities. But as my restaurants prospered, I began to feel a need for somewhere quiet to escape to. So, just outside South Queensferry, about ten miles from Edinburgh, we moved into an empty farmhouse at Bankhead. It became my new obsession.

As there was a great deal to be done we engaged Ferdinand, who seemed able to turn his hand to any task imaginable. I wanted the huge glass greenhouse to be mended, so Ferdinand toiled through the winter, painstakingly removing all the rotting wood and putting in new glass. The house, too, needed urgent attention. Perhaps, after that, I ought to have taken a rest, but no. I had to start on the biggest project of all. I was going to have a successful pottery and it would be in the vast, derelict barn. The idea was my wife Alma's and it seemed ideal as I'd wanted to do something creative and new. So we aimed to have a potters' workshop and studio.

I knew next to nothing about being a potter but that didn't hold me back. After all, there was a time when I knew nothing about running restaurants. Experienced potters warned me of the possible pitfalls but that just made me want to prove them wrong.

It was necessary, first, to find a potter who would share my enthusiasm. I was confident that I would pick up the craft so quickly that after a few months I'd be able to teach the teacher. Meanwhile I'd ordered two brick kilns and half-a-dozen wheels for the workshop.

My imagination rarely rests and I could visualise my students sitting at their wheels, learning in the rustic stone-walled studio. The word would spread and people would come rushing to the farmhouse pottery retreat set amidst soothing trees and fields. The relentless sound of the wheels would be accompanied by birdsong and creative art would prosper amid truly rural peace.

With my imagination firing on all cylinders I got going on producing a brochure to publicise my newest venture. I would have to tempt people away from their dull routines of television and pubs. I would have to entice them to my paradise. Eventually the proofs arrived along with posters which proclaimed: 'Come and see the potters at work in the converted barn and granary overlooking the world-famous Forth Bridges. See a mass of clay transformed on the potter's wheel into a thing of beauty.'

As my ideas began to blossom, so also did life begin to burgeon around me. In the yard, twenty-eight ducks broke free from their shells. To make things even noisier, fifteen baby chicks appeared on the scene almost simultaneously. It was spring. The garden had been tamed and rows of tiny lettuces were poking their heads up through the hard earth. The splashes of green made everything seem just that bit more alive. The yellow daffodils and scarlet tulips added to the awakening landscape. In the greenhouse the first tomato plants were appearing.

I was delighted to see the kilns arrive and I allowed myself another flight of fancy. I imagined all the perfectly finished vases, soup bowls and casserole dishes being carefully removed from the kilns by their ecstatic makers. The works of art would be taken home to living-rooms and kitchens throughout the land to brighten the lives of everyone who saw them. My services to improving the environment would eventually earn me an OBE. I'd be a hero.

The actuality was that the studio was slowly nearing completion in the barn and no one had yet produced one simple pot. We decided to incorporate a tearoom upstairs and a showroom downstairs in order to attract visitors. I didn't want to spend more than I had to, so I contacted a friend in the antique business. I suggested that he might lend me an oak refectory table on which to display my pottery. I was thinking that the table would add class to my wares. My friend was willing to oblige – just as long as his name was featured in such a way that my visitors would be aware where they could get such a table for themselves. I stressed how busy my pottery would be and what a marvellous advertisement it would be for his furniture. Two days later a magnificent table arrived complete with an old-fashioned oil lamp. The showroom was perfect. But I still had to find a potter!

Fortunately a friend came to my aid by telling me about a young man who'd newly finished at Art College and was very keen to make a start somewhere. In fact, he was so eager to start that he was even prepared to work on a trial basis. Shortly afterwards I was introduced to a woman potter who had retired; she was willing to help on a part-time basis.

With these appointments made, I was able to carry on with my plans. I intended to present a 'Pottery Weekend' which would include meals. The highlight would be a candlelit dinner on the Saturday night at the much-talked-of refectory table. I duly placed my adverts in the newspapers, pleasurably anticipating a rush of bookings. But there was a trickle of response rather than a flood; a few hesitant enquiries but no actual bookings.

Was my scheme going to be a disaster? Getting more desperate I sent out brochures to everyone I could think of, but still no bookings came back. After several weeks I could contain myself no longer and decided to do a little market research and phone some of the hesitant inquirers. I asked if my prices seemed too steep. Oh no, that wasn't the problem. They were all quite interested in my pottery weekends but a weekend away was too much to manage. Would a day course or even a morning course be preferable? Yes, was the general opinion. So, I had to rethink my plans.

Somewhat depressed, I wandered upstairs and looked into the comfortable bedrooms lying unused. People didn't know what they were missing, I told myself. Then came the telephone call. Would I be prepared to go on television to be interviewed about my pottery venture? They'd seen one of my brochures and thought

it interesting. Me! On TV! And think of the bookings that would
flood in after the cameras had highlighted the idyllic setting and
the excellent facilities. Then the appalling thought struck me
that, in a pottery, the television people might expect me to make
a pot. And I couldn't. I decided to bluff. For some time I'd been
interested in sculpture and, upstairs in a cupboard, had an
unfinished head. I could set the head on a table and poke about
with it, just like an expert. No one would suspect I hadn't been
spinning the potter's wheel for years.

The television crew arrived. The weather was perfect, dry and
sunny. They put me reasonably at ease and asked me how I
started the venture. The sound of the wheel hummed in the
background as I dabbed and scraped at my actor's prop, the
head. I'd have been less worried had I known what a brief flash in
the evening's entertainment my pottery was going to be. The
well-known face of the programme's host addressed us and there
were my turkeys, ducks and hens gobbling, quacking and clucking
their way around the farmyard. Then came a shot of the old
granary and we heard about a paradise for potters. And there I
was, with my bald patch fully on view for the population of
Scotland to examine. Studiously, I played around with my year-
old piece of sculpture. Luckily, I'd remembered to dust it.

Surely, I would now get a rush of applications. But no, my
hopes were confounded again when I received three or four
inquiries followed by an ominous silence. I began to worry about
how I could keep going when I had no money coming in, and bills
to pay out. I had one other hope – the tearoom upstairs which I
hadn't yet succeeded in getting finished. I'd run restaurants
successfully, so what I had to do now was get my tearoom open
and advertise it. That ought to bring in the customers.

So I produced an eye-catching sign proclaiming, 'Tearoom
This Way', set out an exhibition of pottery from all over the
country, then set out another exhibition – of strawberry tarts.
The people came but they didn't buy the pottery; they rushed for
the strawberry tarts and coffee. In a final despairing attempt to

make the visitors concentrate on the pottery. I increased the price of the tarts. Next day we sold more than ever.

So, in the end, I had my house and my pottery but there seemed no way to make a successful business out of them. I stood in the garden. By then it was July and the summer flowers were out. In the greenhouse the tendrils of the tomato plants were reaching towards the glass roof. In the evening some friends came and stayed. We drank wine at the old refectory table and as it got dark the oil lamp projected our shadows onto the white walls. I was managing to get over my disappointment.

CHAPTER TWENTY-SIX

My Pipe-Dream

The pottery wasn't a success but the house and its surroundings gave me a taste for country living. I remember how my father always seemed to enjoy travelling in the Scottish countryside; it was his advancing years that finally confined him to the city.

My own rural interests expanded a long way away from my father's early days of bartering for chickens and eggs. I eventually had some five hundred birds of my own and a potato-processing plant outside Edinburgh. Then we travelled further afield to Milton Morenish in Perthshire and I got involved in rearing Highland cattle near Loch Tay. I became extremely used to the smells of the farmyard. And it was while in Perthshire that I had my next pipe-dream.

Nowadays you can walk into any British supermarket and choose from a wide range of Scottish, English and French mineral waters. But anyone who has lived as long as I have should know that mineral water used to be bought by only an eccentric handful of people, including those who had been to France on holiday and a few who were frightened of drinking tap water.

In those less enlightened days my Highland home, like many Scottish Highland homes, had its water piped straight into the house from a clear mountain spring. We knew it tasted good but we didn't think a lot about it. Then one day I met a Frenchman. In Germany. I was on my way to a conference at Wolfsburg, travelling by coach from Hanover airport. Sitting beside me was the Frenchman, a complete stranger. He was based in London but was travelling all over Europe, 'in French wine', as they say. We discovered we were both interested in meditation. Soon we were talking non-stop.

While we were discussing healthy minds in healthy bodies, the conversation flowed round to the topic of drinking-water. I was surprised at the interest shown in my own water supply by a man whom I expected would only be interested in drinks that were château-bottled. Then I saw what he was getting at. Why not bottle my mineral spring water and send it all round the globe? In other words, I could export the stuff I normally used for having a shower or washing the dishes.

The bus hurtled through the German countryside but my thoughts weren't concerned with the views from the windows; I was imagining a bottling plant in the Scottish hills with my very own water pouring into bottles by the thousand. And the money! The idea was so incredibly simple that I wondered why I hadn't thought of it myself.

Meantime my new friend was becoming almost incoherent with excitement and was lapsing into a torrent of incomprehensible French. I waited for him to calm down and revert to English. After a while he did, but his eyes were bright and he began to carry me along relentlessly. Had he been a cold businessman obsessed with profit margins, I mightn't have been so interested. But as he was interested in health, meditation and yoga, I thought we might be able to work as a team.

One thing I didn't mention on the bus was that the Department of Health had been testing my water and were considering adding fluoride, chlorine and other substances to my pure mountain spring. Living where I did, I thought I was well away from all forms of pollution. But what, I was warned, if a careless sheep tumbled into my stream, somewhere quiet and unnoticed? Think of the germs I'd be drinking. But my French friend didn't want to know about dead sheep. He was much too alive to the possibility that millions of city-bred types were waiting for the purest Scottish water to filter through to their favourite bars, where it could be mixed with their favourite Scotch. Perhaps, I thought, the drinkers might even prefer my water to the whisky. There could be bars serving only mineral water, and mine would be the favourite brand.

I began to consider a label for my bottles. What would be suitable? I visualised a Highland piper with his cheeks puffed out. That was an image which would be recognisable almost anywhere around the world. Behind him was a waterfall cascading down the heather-clad mountainside. How about a stag, antlers bristling, in the distance? Or a few Highland cattle?

I wondered about depicting a bottle of whisky on my label. This could mean that my water would appeal to spirit drinkers as well as health enthusiasts. The two markets were not incompatible. Anyway, my water was good Scottish stuff and I was becoming convinced that the world was in need of it, complete with a tartan screw-top.

But dreaming about waterfalls and pipers wasn't going to overcome the many technical problems in the scheme. My friend, however, seemed to have it all worked out. We would set up a bottling plant. What we needed was an old barn in which to instal a rotary-type machine. Well, there were enough old barns. We would also need an underground pipe leading straight to the source of the stream (thus taking care of the dead sheep). The water was there, waiting for us. With all the rainfall there in Scotland, we'd never run out. Enough pure water would pour from our pipe to satisfy the thirst of the world.

The venture would fit perfectly with my views on nutrition. With my Farmhouse restaurants in Edinburgh and Glasgow, I'd striven towards providing 'real' food. Now I would be able to put my own natural spring water on the menu as the ideal accompaniment. My French friend promised to visit me. My lack of French could have been a problem but I was lucky to have Vivien Collingwood as next-door neighbour. She spoke French and would help disentangle us if discussions became difficult.

Before parting, we had a brief exchange about finance. 'How much do you think all this will cost?' I asked.

'Oh,' he said, stroking his chin. 'At a rough estimate, £10,000 for the machines.'

'That's not so bad,' I said, wondering to myself, 'Who'll pay out this £10,000?'

'And,' he went on, 'I would say a further £10,000 for bottles, labour and initial distribution.'

Already the price had doubled and I hadn't even left the bus station. Back in Scotland, I decided to do some market research. I slipped into a few big hotels in Edinburgh and asked if there were ever requests for Scottish mineral water. I got the impression that there *was* a potential market. Also, I wrote to acquaintances abroad and asked if they'd ever heard of bottled Scottish water. I half hoped my letters might inspire a few initial orders. They didn't.

One day I was walking, still with spring water on the brain, along Edinburgh's graceful George Street with its many finance houses, insurance offices and banks. I stopped when I noticed the newly-opened branch of the French bank, Crédit Lyonnais. I knew that the manager there was a friend of a friend, so decided to make an appointment. Who better than a Frenchman to appreciate the finer qualities of mineral water, and to have money to lend me?

It turned out, however, that the manager was as British as I am, and he knew nothing about the possibilities of selling mineral water in France or anywhere else. We talked for a bit, but when he got to his feet and stretched out his hand, the way bank managers do, I knew he wasn't going to hand me £20,000. But he did say he might be interested later, once I'd got my scheme off the ground. I must admit I was becoming disillusioned especially as my Frenchman had failed to turn up.

That summer was an unusual one in Scotland: the sun shone and there was little rainfall. It was the first time we'd experienced such weather at the farm. The tap water was reduced to a sorry trickle. As there was barely enough for us, how was I going to slake the thirst of the world from my little spring? Reluctantly, I concluded that my French friend's scheme was a non-starter. Who on earth could make a success out of bottling Scottish water? Not me, I decided.

Now, as I look back, I feel a twinge of regret at my lack of persistence because, subsequently, mineral water companies have set up extremely lucrative businesses in Scotland.

CHAPTER TWENTY-SEVEN

The Rest Farm

Edinburgh, with its international arts festival, attracts many visitors every year. Restaurants do a roaring trade and I find I have little time to myself until the end of September. Then I invariably notice that I am exhausted. That's when I think of holidays and revitalising therapies. And that's when, one year, I decided to investigate the delights of a rest farm.

Such farms invite to their doors the stressed, the strained and the fat. I, of course, was none of these things but I'm willing to try anything once if I think it might recharge my faltering batteries. I made up my mind to undergo a few days of therapy at a rest farm amidst the gentle hills of Hampshire; I'll call the place Greenbourne Hall. There were extensive grounds and a lake as well as all the devices necessary for instant rejuvenation. Although Greenbourne was called a farm, it didn't smell like any farm I'd been on before; it smelt of money.

At the registration desk I was told off for being late. 'You won't be able to see a doctor until Saturday,' the receptionist said in a tone which suggested that it served me right. Even the black-suited porter, as he carried my case upstairs, made me feel like a big useless dog running at his heels.

In my room I looked instantly for the bath or shower. None. I bristled when I thought of the price I was paying, but my indignation decreased when I discovered that Greenbourne Hall, though its bedrooms were bathless, had water wherever it was possible to have a jacuzzi, sauna, treatment room, heated pool or therapeutic bath. There was just no need to bother with ablutions in the privacy of your room.

At dinner there was the choice of a 'normal' or 'diet' menu. I played safe by ordering the 'normal' but was served some steamed fish and vegetables in a portion about the size of a starter. And apart from lemon juice, that was it. I was lucky to be joined by a young couple interested in food. We reminisced about great meals we'd eaten, and managed at least to give our minds a feast.

Afterwards I attended a lecture and was surprised to find myself the only man present at a demonstration of flower arranging. I sat with my tummy rumbling as a tall, thin lady fiddled with twigs and dried leaves. After some forty minutes of her botanical banter, I coughed and said, 'Excuse me, but I understood that tonight's talk was to be called "How To Stay Healthy".'

The lady fixed me with a stare that would have withered a wisteria at twenty yards. 'That talk was cancelled,' she announced coldly. 'The lecturer is ill.'

Back in my room at 8.45 pm I was supposed to retire to bed, but God, I was hungry! In desperation I rummaged in my shoulder-bag and found four dusty pieces of treacle toffee. I sucked and chewed the sticky lumps, feeling all the time like a sinner beyond redemption.

The regime continued next day with fruit for breakfast and salad for lunch. I finished my carrot juice and made my way to the doctor at the appointed hour. I was disturbed at the way his eyebrows shot up when I told him my age. 'You really should try to come here more often,' he said gently, then dismissed me.

I shuffled round the house in my dressing-gown and slippers, stopping off to leap breathlessly up and down with a roomful of women in tights, while a disco beat threatened the foundations. A tuck-in of low-fat cheese and crispbread followed, and I felt revived enough for a leisurely swim. The heated pool with its views of the trees and the golf course was a delight, but I couldn't help watching a very old and dessicated man in huge flappy swimming-trunks who was tremulously undergoing his first swimming lesson. He looked at least 120, and I found myself worrying that this lesson might be his last. I left him there, suspended in the shallow end; I was sure the pockets of air in his swimming-trunks were keeping him afloat.

A place like Greenbourne Hall can do a lot for the body, but I gradually realised that most of the guests were women who had come for beauty treatment, hairdressing and general pampering. They paid to be the centre of attention and loved every self-indulgent second of it. Of course, I would never be so gullible. Or would I?

One evening the director gave us a talk on caring for one's body. When he'd finished, we wanted to ask questions. Disappointingly, he seemed unwilling to provide answers and soon dashed off, perhaps to mull over his accounts. I happened to mention that I ran restaurants dedicated to healthy eating and a lively discussion was soon underway. I took the chair and was soon answering all the questions put by the enthusiastic audience. Yes, my carry-out service was popular. Yes, I displayed notices stating the numbers of calories in meals. Why didn't I open up such a restaurant in London? On and on went the questions, with me thoroughly enjoying myself. Later, back in my bedroom, I realised the discussion was the best part of my visit. Why? Well, like the ladies in the beauty parlour, I'd been the centre of attraction. Just for a little while. And it had done me no end of good.

CHAPTER TWENTY-EIGHT

Pâtisserie Perfection

It is often said that the French and the Scots have much in common. Remember the Auld Alliance. Both races have a definite taste for alcohol and neither is traditionally keen on its mutual neighbours, the English. But when it comes to restaurants, there is no doubt that the French have the better reputation.

Some years ago, I decided to do my own little bit towards making Scottish fare more interesting. I wanted to bring something of Paris to Edinburgh. The Scots are notorious for having a sweet tooth, with a taste for sponge cakes, iced buns, shortbread and vanilla cakes. Most Scottish bakers produce these items remarkably well, but I wanted to do better. Having been to Paris, I'd noticed you could hardly promenade along a rue or boulevard without passing the window display of at least one pâtisserie. And the patterns and colours! The Louvre and The Pompidou Centre had to wait as I stood drooling at the sheer art of the culinary concoctions.

It was late in October when I decided to take a trip to Paris and bring back some examples of the pâtissier's art. I took with me a suitable suitcase and went from shop to shop, buying the most succulent items I could see. No, I wasn't cracking up. I had an idea. I was going to open Edinburgh's first pâtisserie, in Princes Street. The Scottish sweet tooth would guarantee my success and, with Edinburgh Castle opposite my premises, the tourists would flock in as well. But first I had to learn how to make the stuff, and so caused amazement as I carefully placed all my delicate tarts and pastries in my case.

The only part of the operation which had me worried was getting my haul through customs. I could imagine the reaction when my case was opened to reveal dozens of goodies. Would they believe my story or would they suspect that the French Connection was operating again and I'd devised a new way of smuggling heroin or cocaine? Fortunately, I strode through the 'Nothing To Declare' channel without raising suspicion.

Feeling like a schoolboy planning a midnight feast, I arrived back in Edinburgh. But my portable pâtisserie was not for eating, I regret to say. As a restaurateur, I employed my own baker and he was a necessary participant in my plans. I contacted him immediately; it was important not to delay.

Together, we made a forensic examination of each pâtisserie. It was sticky work, but I was determined to uncover the inner secrets of every last delicacy. With magnifying glass and tweezers in hand, we tirelessly dissected the specimens until they yielded up their ingredients of butter, flour, honey, fruit, spices or whatever. We worked with the undivided attention and concentration of two brain surgeons. Then, as we concocted our versions of the originals, we were like two counterfeiters, intent on fooling the art world with our reproductions. There was sifting and beating, baking and tasting. And after the tasting, there was rejection if we hadn't managed to match the French originals. In time, I believe we actually produced some results which surpassed the originals. I know because I tasted the lot.

Meanwhile, in Princes Street, part of my restaurant was being converted into a pâtisserie. The joiners were building a brightly-lit counter, with display shelves facing the pavement. On the eve of the opening, a tantalising window display was set out. It was so convincing I almost thought I smelt Gauloises and garlic from the breaths of passers-by. It was so eye-catching that hundreds of people stopped to examine our mouth-watering morsels through the glass. But would they buy when we opened? I'm never free from doubts, but this time I needn't have worried. Everything was soon sold. The Auld Alliance was obviously still alive and well and the Scots bought up my French delicacies as fast as we could produce them.

CHAPTER TWENTY-NINE

Primal Scream

Restaurants continue to involve me; at the time of writing, I'm seventy-two and happily married, but 'retirement' is absent from my thoughts. In fact, I'm planning a working trip to New York.

Also, I'm still fascinated by such things as alternative medicine, therapy and meditation, and I'd like to close this volume with an experience which, in a way, took me right back to my beginnings, to my schooldays and St Leonard's Hill.

One of the therapies I investigated in the hope of learning to understand myself better was the Primal Scream method associated with Dr Arthur Janov. I drifted into it quite casually, unaware of what an unsettling experience lay ahead. It is, as I understand it, a process which allows us to release the traumatic emotions which we keep bottled up inside ourselves. The treatment involves returning, in the mind, to childhood in order to discover the cause of our distress. Ideally, once the traumatic experience has been pinpointed, a mental block is removed and you are free to continue your emotional and psychological development.

The treatment is sometimes carried out in a group session where other participants may act out the roles of parents, friends or whoever. There is a deliberate build-up of tension as you are encouraged to re-enact the original damaging experience. The climax comes when you are urged to release the tension in a way which wasn't possible the first time. Sometimes the treatment will end in tears, screams or both.

I was personally unable to pinpoint any one particularly traumatic incident in my younger days, but I was willing to undergo the treatment in the hope that it might lead me to a more peaceful state of mind. I know that my father with his stinging leather strap upset and hurt me but, at that time, it was reasonably common for fathers to beat their children and I don't think that my treatment was exceptional. I suspected that there might be a skeleton in my cupboard, waiting to be discovered and released; if there were, I wanted to come face to face with it.

The man who, perhaps, held the key was an eccentric Pole who lived in London. I'll call him Jack. He had long wished to hold a session in Scotland but his organisation had no permanent premises north of the Border. He couldn't just hire any old room. As the sessions invariably involved distressing cries of rage and anguish, any accommodation had to be suitably soundproofed.

At the time, I had a flat situated two floors above an old restaurant. Much of the block was unlived in, so there was no need to worry about neighbours. I offered the flat to Jack for a group session and he was delighted to accept; it would give him a chance to enrol some Scottish disciples.

We decided to have the meeting at a weekend, to let as many people as possible attend. My door stood open and in came the expectant crowd. There were students, a housewife, an economist, a computer analyst and a sprinkling of unworldly characters in saffron robes: they were the followers of an Indian guru and, although as Scottish as Rabbie Burns, they had names like Sashkavananda and Mahachakavishnu. I could tell it was not going to be an ordinary day.

Jack, of course, was in charge of the session, and we began by sitting or lying around listening to classical music. This was to relax us and allow us to bring our emotions more to the surface. The music, which was obviously carefully chosen, was powerful. One moment I felt I was being helplessly seduced by enchanting Rhinemaidens; then I was lying in some perfect Eden, intoxicated by the scents of unknown flowers, lulled by the humming of bees and the silvery sound of tumbling streams. This was good. My sense of relaxation vanished, however, when Jack suddenly suggested that we'd be more comfortable if we disposed of any encumbering clothes which might prevent us from moving freely.

I was wondering whether to remove my tie and socks when I became aware, all about me, of the rustling of cotton and nylon, the rattling of buckles, the sudden flashing of liberated white flesh. The trappings of civilisation were being removed. Had I, unsuspectingly, handed over my flat for an orgy? However, the striptease only went so far, and the men retained their dignity in their Y-fronts while the women, looking like a page of adverts in a mail-order catalogue, sat around in their bras and briefs. In an onrush of enthusiasm, however, the computer analyst had stripped himself completely. Realising he was alone in his all-revealing innocence, he sheepishly slipped back into his Y-fronts. I was interested to learn that the Indian guru's followers had nothing holier than ordinary underwear beneath their robes.

The next stage was the massage. We were put into pairs and tackled each other's bodies with vigour. This, too, helped to break down our everyday barriers, but it felt odd to be in such close physical contact with someone whom, an hour earlier, I would have walked past in the street.

Then the real treatment began. A young man volunteered to tell us all about his pet hates and hang-ups. To me, he didn't sound as if he had any problems worth bothering about, but I suppose that the person I *really* wanted to find out about was me. The next young man was a Jew and his distress appeared to have arisen from the occasion of his circumcision. The dramatic possibilities of this soon had Jack leaping around to get us all organised. The whole story was to be acted out but we needed a villain for the piece. Who was going to play the part of the rabbi? All eyes came to rest on me and I was unanimously voted into the role of knife-wielder. I decided to make the most of my star part. The poor young man was laid out on the floor and amid much noise and gesturing we went through the ritual, making it, as far as we could, a grisly ordeal. I brought the knife down and skilfully mimed the final cut. The young man began by whimpering and blubbering, then began to scream. I like to hope it did him some good.

It wasn't too long before it was my turn for treatment. I felt as if I were in the spotlight and had omitted to prepare a party piece. Desperately, I raked through the murkier recesses of my memory. In the end, I told the group about the embarrassment which I used to suffer in my schooldays because I had a weak bladder. In all honesty, I didn't regard the matter as serious but I felt I had to say *something*.

Because of my Jewishness, I often felt like an outsider at school and, naturally, the last thing I wanted was to draw attention to myself. So, whenever I needed to go to 'the lavvies', I just used to sit tight and say nothing; I was too frightened to put my hand up and ask the teacher. I can remember the agonies as I wriggled about on the hard seat and crossed and uncrossed my legs. I would try to concentrate on my sums or spelling, but all I could think of was the agonising pressure. At the end of the day, I would rush from school, through the streets, up the stairs and into the dark sanctuary of the family toilet.

But, as I informed the therapy group, on one occasion it had all become too much for me. The dam had finally burst and my defences were left in ruins. I can't remember what the lesson was at the time. I was concentrating all my efforts on the pressure between my legs. I winced and sweated, wondering how long it could be until the bell rang. The teacher noticed my unusual behaviour

'What's the matter with you, boy? Have you got ants in your pants?' she asked. Glad of any interruption in the lessons, the rest of the class tittered.

'No, miss,' I said, hoping to be left in peace. She turned back to the blackboard and then it happened. A warm torrent welled from my trousers onto the dusty floor. Steaming, it spread round my shoes, out from my desk and down the aisle. The class erupted into scornful laughter. Wee Hymie peeing on the floor was the undoubted highlight of the week. The teacher managed some embarrassed tutting and I was sent home in disgrace to get changed.

The group listened to my tragic tale in silence. As soon as I'd finished, Jack was on his feet and getting us all organised. As the star of the show, I had to lie on the floor with my hand gripping my penis. Concentrating as hard as I could, I tried to bring back the unfriendly atmosphere of that classroom. I attempted to recall the drone of the teacher's voice. Then Jack broke in and began to describe the scene to me, just as I'd already told it. To my amazement and horror, I found I wanted to pee. I cursed the cup of tea I'd had before the sessions began. Soon, I was no longer play-acting. I was fighting with all my strength to control my bladder. Jack's voice began to sound like the teacher's and I was back in school again, terrified of the inevitable humiliation. At the same time, I was still half-aware that I was lying on my own expensive new carpet and this only added to my anxiety. As the torture became unbearable, a soft feminine voice broke into my consciousness. 'It's all right Hymie,' it said. 'Go on Hymie. Don't worry. Relax. Just let go, relax.' What else could I do? The floodgates opened and with intense relief I soaked my Y-fronts.

I should add that this weird drama took place while others in the group were acting out scenes from their own childhoods. One man was laughing like a maniac; in another corner someone was groaning loudly. I understood these noises to be reactions to what I'd done and in my confusion I yelled, 'Stop it you bastards!'

Eventually, with the soothing assistance of some of the other participants, I calmed down. Jack, with a foresight which amazed me, had been standing by with a big towel, and I was spared a bill for carpet-cleaning. My flat had seemed, at times, like a wing of an asylum but, when all was over, I did have a terrific new sense of well-being. I was impressed.

Before Jack returned to London, I made an appointment to see him for a personal consultation. I thought he might have the answers to my problems. I journeyed south to his tiny basement flat, a damp, peeling hole in Paddington. He had the requisite couch, and I was soon stretched out, telling him about my childhood. He helped me regress, and together we explored episodes in my life where I'd been angered or frustrated. He encouraged me to pound my fists on a cushion, as a means of release. His next step was to suggest that he was responsible for the things that had gone wrong with my life, and I could attack him with the cushion. This would, he assured me, bring the peace of mind I sought.

I got up from the couch and swung the cushion at his left shoulder. Then, swearing heartily, I laid into Jack for a full ten minutes as he ducked and dodged around his scruffy little room.

'What are you thinking about?' he asked, still trying to keep up the treatment.

'I am thinking,' I replied breathlessly, 'why am I paying £10 for a pillow fight?'

'What else?' Jack asked.

'That I ought to see a psychiatrist.'

'What else?' he persisted.

'That you're a bloody charlatan and must be laughing all the way to the bank,' I gasped as I swung the cushion hard into the side of his head.

That was my final opinion of Jack. I never changed it. He was a chancer, but a clever one.

*   *   *

I suppose there were times in my life when I myself must have seemed a chancer. Should I have claimed, all those years ago, to have been an experienced aerial photographer? Should I have tried to sell tartan scrolls to the Americans? Should I have let that cardinal believe I was a portrait painter?

I do know that having been out on my own at the age of fourteen I had to learn to take chances whenever they came along. That's why I seem to have had so many different careers. My life has been a search for an occupation I could live with. I gave up a successful career in photography. Now I'm a restaurateur. The Farmhouses came and went, and now I'm enjoying

169

running one large restaurant in Edinburgh. Also, I'm still working at relaxation. I like writing and playing bridge, and have recently taken up the guitar.

Like my father, I have always been an entrepreneur. Like him, I followed a road which was often solitary. I was always searching for new business ventures, but at the same time I wanted to develop personally. It was never a need for financial rewards which drove me on. It was, perhaps, a deep sense of inadequacy. On the other hand, it could be I was driven by vanity, an unwillingness to admit to limitations.

For many years I have been fascinated by ideas, philosophies and religions. Perhaps the loss of my Jewish faith left a space to be filled. Now, in my seventies, I continue to work. In my restarurant I provide wholesome food, made from natural ingredients. I try to use organically-grown vegetables and organically-produced meat. The eggs are free-range; colouring and preservatives are outlawed. I don't wish merely to fill people with food and make a profit. I want them to become healthier, happier human beings.

I am a believer in the phrase: you are what you eat. And I think my beliefs can be traced back to my mother's kitchen at St Leonard's Hill, and also perhaps those ancient Jewish dietary laws. (Yes, we do serve chicken in my restaurant, but I don't have to carry a sackful of the frantic birds through the streets to the butcher's!)

I continue my searching: books on philosophy and recipe books lie side by side on my desk. I'll never put on a pair of slippers and settle down by the fireside. My father never did.